Henry James:
The Later Novels

Twayne's United States Authors Series

David J. Nordloh, Editor

Indiana University at Bloomington

TUSAS 521

HENRY JAMES
(1843–1916)
Photograph by permission of
the Houghton Library,
Harvard University.

Henry James:
The Later Novels

By William R. Macnaughton

University of Waterloo, Ontario

Twayne Publishers
A Division of G.K. Hall & Co. • *Boston*

Henry James: The Later Novels
William R. Macnaughton

Copyright 1987 by G.K. Hall & Co.
All rights reserved.
Published by Twayne Publishers
A Division of G.K. Hall & Co.
70 Lincoln Street
Boston, Massachusetts 02111

Copyediting supervised by Lewis DeSimone
Book production by Kristina Hals
Book design by Barbara Anderson

Typeset in 11 pt. Garamond
by Compset, Inc., of Beverly, Massachusetts

Printed on permanent/durable acid-free paper
and bound in the United States of America

Library of Congress Cataloging in Publication Data

Macnaughton, William R., 1939–
Henry James : the later novels.

(Twayne's United States authors series ; TUSAS 521)
Bibliography: p.
Includes index.
1. James, Henry, 1843–1916—Criticism and
interpretation. I. Title. II. Series.
PS2124.M267   1987   813'.4   87-15030
ISBN 0-8057-7505-6

Contents

About the Author

William R. Macnaughton received his B.A. from the University of Toronto and M.A. and Ph.D. from the University of Wisconsin. He has taught at and been chairman of the English Department at the University of Waterloo in Waterloo, Ontario, Canada. He is the author of *Mark Twain's Last Years as a Writer* (1979), editor of *Critical Essays on John Updike* (1982), and author of many essays and reviews appearing in American and Canadian publications.

Preface

In his preface to *Henry James: The Early Novels,* published as part of this series in 1983, Robert Emmet Long conjectures that, because of the vast amount of secondary literature on James, what the reader "might like to have at the present time is a single volume . . . that consolidates this scholarship and brings the novels themselves into clear focus—the objectives of this study." Because the scholarship devoted to the later novels is even more daunting, the objectives of this volume are similar. Similar also is the audience for which I intend it: general readers with some interest in James and American literature specialists. My volume also attempts to offer "original readings and observations, rather than a summary of what has already been said." Thus, readers will find here, for example, an unconventionally positive evaluation of *The Tragic Muse*; an analysis of *The Ambassadors* stressing the importance of sexuality and action (not passivity) to Lambert Strether; an interpretation of *The Wings of the Dove* explaining the benefits deriving from James's loss of conscious control of the narrative; a view of *The Golden Bowl* emphasizing his competitive drive to improve upon certain European writers and his own earlier work. The general picture of James emerging from this study is also mildly iconoclastic: of a writer who could never completely give up his desire for financial success and a large, heterogeneous audience; and of an author who often wrote best as a servant of the creative process rather than as a controlled, conscious Master.

A final similarity between these two Twayne books is the format of each major chapter: an opening focusing on background to the novel, with important earlier scholarship succinctly summarized; a section discussing the texts and the critical reception of each novel (this information is sometimes given in a note); and—the most significant part of the chapter—a lengthy critical interpretation.

An important difference between these Twayne books derives from my belief that a novel is a realistic prose fiction significantly longer than some works (*The Europeans,* for example) discussed by Professor Long. For the purposes of my study, I define a James novel as a completed work to which at least one volume in James's New York Edition is devoted; I allot most space to this fiction. Works written during these years such as *The Reverberator, The Spoils of Poynton, What Maisie Knew, The Turn of the Screw, In the Cage, The Sacred Fount,* and *The Outcry* I call novellas and discuss only as they relate to the long structures.

One reason for this definition is that it reflects James's own attitude as revealed in a 30 July 1905 memorandum to Charles Scribner's Sons about the organization of his New York Edition.[1] A further reason is pragmatic: my wish to do justice to the complexity of the late novels and the sometimes brilliant criticism inspired by them.

In preparing this book, I have benefited greatly from the work of earlier James scholars, some of whom are cited in the annotated bibliography. Particularly helpful, of course, have been Leon Edel's publications, especially the five-volume and one-volume biographies, the bibliography of James's writings, and the four-volume edition of the letters. I am indebted, for the use of their research facilities, to the main libraries at the University of Waterloo and Indiana University, and to the latter's excellent Lilly Library. In addition, I owe large thanks, for their financial support, to the SSHRC, and to the Arts Faculty and English Department of the University of Waterloo. I also wish to thank four colleagues: Walter Martin and Warren Ober, for their interest in this project and informed love of James, and Eric McCormack and Sean Virgo, for their good-natured skepticism. Finally, I want to dedicate this book to Liz, for her initial encouragement, and to Emily, who has not read Henry James, but who will, some day.

William R. Macnaughton

University of Waterloo

Chronology

1843	Henry James, Jr., born in New York City on 15 April, second of five children of Henry James, Sr., and Mary Walsh James.
1882	Mother dies in late January, father on 20 December.
1883	August, returns to London after duties as executor of father's estate. Death of Ivan Turgenev. *The Seige of London* (stories), *Portraits of Places* (travel essays), and fourteen-volume collected edition of his fiction.
1884	February, visits Paris and meets again Daudet, Zola, and Edmund de Goncourt. Alice James arrives in England in late 1884. September, "The Art of Fiction" in *Longman's Magazine* leads to friendship with R.L. Stevenson. *A Little Tour in France* and *Tales of Three Cities* (stories).
1885	*The Author of "Beltraffio"* (stories) and *Stories Revived, 3* volumes. *The Bostonians* serialized in *Century*. *The Princess Casamassima* serialized in the *Atlantic*.
1886	March, moves into De Vere Gardens. Bothered by civil and political unrest. *The Bostonians* and *The Princess Casamassima* issued as books.
1887	Visits Italy until July and sees much of Constance Fenimore Woolson. Writes literary criticism and short fiction. Asked in December to prepare stage version of *The American*.
1888	*Partial Portraits* (criticism), *The Reverberator* (novella), *The Aspern Papers* (short stories).
1889	*The Tragic Muse* serialized in the *Atlantic*. *A London Life* (stories) and *Port Tarascon* (translation of novel by Daudet). Visits Italy and Germany.
1890	Decides to write plays and short fiction. Hires literary agent. *The Tragic Muse*.
1891	Sees first Ibsen play (*A Doll's House*). Visits Ireland. *The American* is performed in London (fall). Death of James Russell Lowell and Wolcott Balestier.

1892   Alice James dies 9 March. Visits Italy. *The Lesson of the Master* (stories).

1893   Visits William in Lausanne. *The Real Thing and Other Tales, Pictures and Texts* (essays), *The Private Life* (stories), *Essays in London and Elsewhere, The Wheel of Time* (stories).

1894   Death (probable suicide) of Constance Woolson in Venice, 24 January. Visits Italy. *Theatricals* (plays).

1895   5 January, *Guy Domville* opens; closes after forty performances. Begins work on longer fiction. *Terminations* (stories).

1896   Summer near Rye; discovers Lamb House. Late in year begins to dictate work. *Embarrassments* (stories) and *The Other House* (novella based on play).

1897   Leases, then buys Lamb House. *The Spoils of Poynton* (novella) and *What Maisie Knew* (novella).

1898   *The Awkward Age* serialized in *Harper's Weekly*. *In the Cage* (novella) and *The Two Magics* ("The Turn of the Screw" and "Covering End," originally a one-act play).

1899   Visits France and Italy. Meets young sculptor, Henrik Andersen. Hires James Pinker as agent. *The Awkward Age*.

1900   Writes furiously in late 1899 and early 1900 to help pay off Lamb House. Shaves off beard (June). Takes room at Reform Club (fall). *The Soft Side* (stories).

1901   Visit of brother's family and William's Edinburgh lectures. Employs typist who types directly from dictation. Fires alcoholic servants. *The Sacred Fount* (novella).

1902   Health problems early in year. Disposes of lease on De Vere Gardens. *The Wings of the Dove* (no serialization). Meets Jocyln Persse and Edith Wharton.

1903   *The Ambassadors* serialized in *North American Review*. *The Better Sort* (stories), *The Ambassadors* (written before *The Wings of the Dove*), *William Wetmore Story and His Friends*.

1904   August, returns to America after twenty-one years. *The Golden Bowl* (no serialization).

1905   Travels, lectures in America. August, travels to England. *The Question of Our Speech, English Hours* (essays).

1907   Summer, motor trip in France with Whartons. Hires Theodora Bosanquet as amanuensis. *The American Scene* (impressions); New York Edition, 24 volumes; two posthumous volumes added, 1917.

1908   Visit of William James family. *The High Bid* performed in Edinburgh (March) and London (February 1909). Writing for theater.

1909   Poor sales of New York Edition confirmed. Illness late in year. *Italian Hours* (essays).

1910   Illness continues. Theaters closed because of king's death and *The Outcry* not performed. Accompanies William Jameses to William's summer home in New Hampshire. William dies 26 August. *The Finer Grain* (stories).

1911   January, one-act *The Saloon* performed in London. Spring, honorary degree conferred by Harvard. August, returns to England. Edith Wharton tries unsuccessfully to have Nobel Prize awarded to James. *The Outcry* (novella based on play).

1912   June, honorary degree conferred by Oxford. Request for American novel by Scribner's (secretly arranged by Edith Wharton).

1913   Seventieth birthday honored by friends with commission of portrait by John Sargent. *A Small Boy and Others* (autobiography).

1914   Outbreak of war. *Notes of a Son and Brother* (autobiography), *Notes on Novelists*.

1915   Work on behalf of war effort, on novels, on preface to book by Rupert Brooke. *The Tales of Henry James*, 14 volumes.

1916   January, Order of Merit conferred. James dies 28 February.

1917   *The Ivory Tower, The Sense of the Past, The Middle Years* (two novels and autobiography).

1919   *Within the Rim and Other Essays* (wartime essays).

Chapter One

Introduction:
James at Midcareer

In the winter of 1885 Henry James was forty-one years old, had been publishing since 1864, and was now living permanently in London, in downtown Bolton Street, after having abandoned a brief desire to purchase a comfortable and commodious house in St. John's Wood. Both parents had recently died, as had his younger brother Wilky, who had never been in good health after a Civil War injury. James had been in England for more than a year, after having completed his duties in America as executor of his father's estate (and conceived the idea for *The Bostonians,* which had just begun serialization in the *Century Magazine,* and upon which he was hard at work).

Surviving in James's immediate family were his younger brother Robertson (with whom James would never be close); and his older brother, William—rival and friend—now a family man and on his way at Harvard to establishing a reputation as one of the great philosopher-psychologists of the century; and his younger sister, Alice—bright, frustrated, unhappy, and ill—unable to find an outlet for her talents in the essentially masculine worlds of the James family and nineteenth-century United States. James had recently witnessed her grotesque disembarkment on a stretcher from her ship in Liverpool. Since that time he had arranged accommodation for Alice in London, but currently she was living at the seaside health resort of Bournemouth with her friend and nurse, Katharine Loring, and her sister, Louisa, who had weak lungs. Alice was noticeably jealous of Louisa, but fortunately her health was improving, and she soon returned to the United States.

Although James's house-hunting had encouraged a few friends to imagine matrimony for the attractive bachelor, he had vowed that he would never marry, primarily, it seemed, because he did not think he could reconcile successfully the vocation of marriage and the profession of authorship, both of which he took seriously. Despite his pledge, however, he had many female friends in America, England, and on the

1

Continent. One of his closest (almost uncomfortably so) present relations was with the American writer Constance Fenimore Woolson—
the restless and homeless grandniece of James Fenimore Cooper—who
was an intense admirer of James's work and person, and who had taken
up temporary residence in London.

Among the several other friendships he had begun to cultivate were
those with the artist-illustrator George Du Maurier, best-known for
his work with *Punch* (and later for the incredibly popular novel *Trilby*);
the successful novelist Mrs. Humphry Ward and her husband, who was
an editor of the *Times*; the charming, gossipy civil servant and man of
letters Edmund Gosse (probably James's best friend throughout this
period) and his wife; the vital, although tubercular, novelist living at
Bournemouth, Robert Louis Stevenson, who had written a "Humble
Remonstrance" to James's recently published "Art of Fiction," and
whose amiable overtures soon led to a relation significant to both men
until Stevenson's premature death; John Sargent, the young American
expatriate artist whom James had met in France the previous winter
and who was now, in part because of James's suggestion, living in
London and developing a reputation; and Paul Bourget, a young
French writer whom Sargent had introduced to James in the summer
and whose novella (*Cruelle Énigme*) had been dedicated to him and soon
made Bourget famous in France. James did not really like Bourget's
fiction (a response that later became common to the work of his many
acolytes), but found him to be a brilliant talker and enjoyable
company.

James was proud of how his career had developed and confident
about the truth of the principles enunciated eloquently (and idealisti-
cally) in "The Art of Fiction": that authorship was not merely a job or
a source of popular entertainment and pleasant make-believe but a demanding, admirable profession, analogous in ways to the vocations of
historian, philosopher, and artist; that fiction should express the author's vision of life; that great fiction would probably be ethical (since
it was so intimately related to the mind and heart of its creator), but
not narrowly moralistic; that it would, almost certainly (since writers
of fiction were artists), possess formal beauty; that great writers would
be concerned about form (although not in a programmatic or restrictive
way); that worthwhile fiction would challenge its readers and not pander to their lowest and most conventional expectations (such as for
happy endings); that, because of the goals and methods of its creators
and its dynamic relation with its readers, great fiction would be inter-

esting. Perhaps most important, the writer would be free to express her or his own individual picture of life in her or his own particular fashion.

That James at this point in his career was also confident—at least in one part of his mind—of financial success was shown when he decided to give to his sister his father's legacy of $20,000. Several factors had buoyed up this confidence. He had influential literary admirers in England and America—his longtime friend William Dean Howells, for example, former editor of the *Atlantic Monthly,* enthusiastic supporter of James since the beginning of his career and author of an admiring, controversial 1882 article about his fiction. Macmillan of London had thought so highly of his work that it had published in 1883 a fourteen-volume collected edition. James wrote not only novels but also short fiction, criticism, and travel essays with relative ease and published them with remarkable frequency. His reasonably lucrative practice was first to serialize his novels and then to arrange for simultaneous book publication (so as to avoid infringements of copyright) on both sides of the Atlantic. He had recently signed a contract with the *Atlantic Monthly* for a new "London" novel, as yet unnamed, to be serialized in 1885–86 at $15 per page or approximately $350 per month. Although some James admirers were probably young ladies infatuated by the style of life depicted in his fiction and by their image of its sophisticated author, James's reputation among many discriminating readers was excellent: they valued his subtlety and wit, supported his attempts to create a profession of authorship, and were undoubtedly flattered by his respect for their intelligence and sensitivity.

In an 1884 article, Julian Hawthorne (son of the great novelist and himself an author) had compared James to Ivan Turgenev (James's friend and mentor, whom James had eulogized upon his death in 1883), and had written that James (and Howells) "have done more than all the rest of us to make our literature respectable during the last ten years."[1] A little later in the same year Edgar Fawcett, while reviewing *The Portrait of a Lady,* had written an informed and wonderfully appreciative discussion of James's novels that had concluded, "As it is, there is little doubt that he deserves today to be called the first of English-writing novelists" (147). And in a February 1884 visit to Paris James had met again, conversed passionately with, and been recognized and welcomed by a group of French writers (including Alphonse Daudet, Edmond de Goncourt, and Émile Zola), whose attitudes toward literature he found inspiring. For all these reasons, therefore, if he had read Fawcett's encomium in the *Princeton Review,* James would probably have agreed with the critic's prediction: "That he will give us, in the future years which supposedly still await him work of even a stouter fibre against oblivion than any which he has yet produced, is far from improbable" (147).

On the other hand, several signs were not positive. There was the problem of sales, for example: although James's multifarious efforts as man of letters brought a living wage, his books did not sell nearly as well as those of authors he believed inferior.[2] Writing to Howells from Paris in February 1884, James complained, "What you tell me of the success of————'s last novel sickens and almost paralyzes me. It seems to me [the book] is so contemptibly bad and ignoble that the idea of people reading it in such numbers makes one return upon one's self and ask what is the use of trying to write anything decent or serious for a public so absolutely idiotic" (142).

Nor was James's fiction greeted by reviewers with universal approbation. Disturbing, for example, were the enemies created for him by Howells's somewhat chauvinistic (although well-intentioned) suggestion that his friend led a group of writers whose work represented "a finer art . . . that it was with Dickens and Thackeray" (132). Although James to a certain extent appreciated Howells's support, he also was becoming embarrassed by being linked consistently with him—in part because he believed himself to be the better novelist. A complicating factor was that many American reviewers were irritated by James's critical treatment of his country and its citizens in stories such as "The Point of View." To say that many readers believed James to be a snobbish Anglophile turncoat would not be an exaggeration.

If James had read a very recent review in the *Dial* (December 1884), he might have found it particularly disquieting because, the critic had asserted, "it is becoming painfully evident that Mr. James has written himself out as far as the international novel is concerned, and probably as far as any kind of novel-writing is concerned. . . . But style and invention are both becoming old stories already with most of his readers, who are sure to drop off one by one if he cannot hit upon some fresh literary device by which to renew his bond with them" (153). Even if James had not read the review, that he himself had already sensed the need to move away from international fiction was implied by the current *Bostonians.* Moreover, in the letter to Howells he had said that the French "do the only kind of work, today, that I respect"

(142); and that the last novel by Zola was "admirably solid and serious" (143).

Another problem for James, however, was how to reconcile his admiration for the French and his recognition that he must leave international long fiction with his temperamental inability to embrace the "ferocious pessimism" of the naturalists or to handle "unclean things" (142). A further complication was James's strong suspicion that any adoption of French subject matter (sexual relations, for example) or tone might alienate many readers who had bought his earlier fiction. James at forty-one had accomplished a great deal and had large ambitions. Yet how—his roots in America almost torn out, his attachment to his chosen culture tenuous and nonadhesive—was he to grow as a writer and also eat well, entertain comfortably, travel freely, and win discerning—and wide—support for his aims and achievements? In short, how was he to reconcile art with the world?

Chapter Two

The Princess Casamassima: Politics and Culture

Background

Genesis and text. In his preface to the New York Edition of *The Princess Casamassima,* James wrote that "The simplest account of the origin" of the novel was that it "proceeded quite directly, during the first year of a long residence in London, from the habit and the interest of walking the streets."[1] How much of the novel he had imagined during this "first year of a long residence" it is difficult to say, but it is clear from a 12 December 1884 letter to his longtime American friend, Thomas Sergeant Perry, that he had actually begun around that time to collect notes for the first important scene. In the letter James comments on his visit to Millbank Prison, referring to himself somewhat ruefully as "quite the naturalist."[2] By April 1885 James had completed the serialization of *The Bostonians* and, upon moving to his summer home at Bournemouth, he was ready to devote himself to *The Princess Casamassima.* According to a letter of 23 May, he had completed the first installment for the *Atlantic Monthly* by that date. Then, despite some time spent in early July in an eventually successful attempt to locate a home in London for his invalid sister Alice and her companion and nurse, Katharine Loring, he was, according to a 12 August *Notebooks* entry, about to begin working on the third installment. Unlike *The Bostonians,* whose structure he had mapped out well in advance of his work on it—even before leaving the United States, in fact—James at this point in the development of his new novel was not certain about the precise direction it was to take. His notebook confides: "I have never yet become engaged in a novel in which, after I had begun to write and send off my MS., the details had remained so vague."[3]

Despite this fact, James completed both the third and fourth installments before crossing to Paris in early fall to stay at the apartment lodgings where he had resided in 1876 just prior to moving to London. We cannot be certain how long he had planned to remain in Paris, or whether he had, by this point, envisioned the sojourn of his protagonist in the French capital and had wished to write this section while himself living in the city.

Whatever his plans might have been, James was compelled to return to London in late autumn because of a crisis in his sister's health. In large part because of his continuing concern for Alice, James remained in London for almost all of the next thirteen months. In December 1885, as if to symbolize his commitment to his adopted city, he signed a twenty-one year lease for a commodious fourth floor flat with a view, close to the Albert Memorial, in Kensington, in a building called De Vere Gardens into which he finally moved on 6 March 1886.

The months in which he worked on the serialization of *The Princess Casamassima* were marked by comparative domestic tranquillity but also by much social and political unrest. Everywhere were signs of a civilization threatened from within (by poverty, riots, scandals in high places, agitation for Home Rule in Ireland), and without (the brief possibility of war with Russia in Armenia, the disastrous British expeditions led by Colonel Gordon into the Sudan). During the period when James worked on *The Princess Casamassima,* there were three changes in government, as the rickety Liberal party, led by the aged William Gladstone, tried desperately to survive. Writing to his brother William on 9 December 1885, Henry remarks that "Civil War seems to me to be really in the air."

By early July James had dispatched his last installment to the *Atlantic Monthly* (the novel was serialized from September 1885 until October 1886); by early September he had finished minor revisions for the book edition. Writing to his brother on 10 September, he vowed that never again would he create a novel as long as *The Princess.*[4] Macmillan published a three-volume edition of 750 copies on 22 October 1886; and, in the same month, printed 3,000 copies of a cheaper one-volume edition. Some of these copies were published in America in early November 1886; the rest appeared in England in August 1887. In 1888 Macmillan also issued a cheap (two shilling) edition—two printings of 2,000 copies each. Both the issuing of this "yellowback" edition and the generally favorable reviews of the novel suggest *The Princess Casamassima*'s relative popularity.[5] The final version is the New York Edition, for which James made several thousand revisions and chose two photographic frontispieces (of St. Paul's seen from across the

Thames and l'Arc de Triomphe) in collaboration with the young pho-
tographer Alvin Langdon Coburn.[6]

Source and influence. In his nostalgic preface to the New York
Edition, James suggests that the novel's major source was an image
derived from his wanderings in the London streets. The image was of
a person, like the author himself—"some individual sensitive nature
or fine mind . . . capable of profiting by all the civilization, all the
accumulations to which they [the 'humming presences' of the city]
testify"—but who, unlike the author, would be condemned to watch
from "the most respectful of distances and with every door shut in his
face." This ambiguous image of yearning susceptibility and frustrating
privation suggested a question: "of what the total assault, that of the
world of his workaday life and the world of his divination and his envy
together would have made of him, and what in especial he would have
made of them." Eventually, in answering the question, James created
a novel with a "social—not less than socialist—connection." His conclusion is that "I felt in full *personal* possession of my matter; this really
seemed the fruit of direct experience" (1:xxi).

Scholars have suggested many plausible sources for ingredients in
the novel to which the author does not refer. The novel most frequently
and convincingly cited as a crucial source for several facets of *The Princess Casamassima* is Ivan Turgenev's *Virgin Soil,* which James reviewed.
This novel also contains a somewhat passive central character (like Hyacinth Robinson)—the unrecognized natural son of a nobleman—torn
between a vow to commit a terrorist act and sympathy for the class he
must destroy, in love with an upper-class woman, and finally "solving"
his dilemma by suicide. Other resemblances between the two novels
also seem more than accidental: between Turgenev's cool revolutionary
leader (admired by the tergiversating hero) and Paul Muniment, for
example, or between the crippled, aristocratic-loving sister of another
radical in *Virgin Soil* and Rosy Muniment.

Other works that may have influenced the radical element in James's
novel are Flaubert's *L'Éducation Sentimentale,* Dostoevski's *The Possessed,*
various "working class" novels (a flourishing subgenre at the time),
even potboilers such as one by R. L. Stevenson and his wife called *The
Dynamiters* or F. Marion Crawford's *To Leeward.* The influence of Dickens is also evident in characters such as Mrs. Bowerbank and in the
powerful, grotesque scene in the prison to which she leads Pinnie and
Hyacinth; or in Geoffrey Sholto, the jaded aristocrat, whose attitude

toward life reminds one of James Harthouse in *Hard Times*; or in the fiddler (and parental figure) Anastasius Vetch's feeling that life is a "muddle," which suggests Steven Blackpool. One might also argue that James's novel's implied preferences for the particularity of persons over the abstraction of politics and for the life of the imagination over an involvement in social "betterment" are influenced by *Hard Times*.

The probable influence of other specific writers and works is also relatively easy to discern. Adeline Tintner argues, for example, that James's conception of his central character has been influenced by Richard Monk's life of John Keats, the "cockney poet," in such details as class, family background, size, and sensitivity. Both figures, moreover, are sensitive not only to beauty but to the seductiveness of personal extinction, because Hyacinth, like the speaker of "Ode to a Nightingale," is at times "half in love with easeful death." An implicit contrast between the two, one designed to increase the pathos of Hyacinth's predicament, is that Hyacinth as would-be writer remains silent. Joseph Firebaugh has also argued that James's youthful reading of Schopenhauer (who is mentioned several times) has had specific influences on the novel—in the harmful effect of the women on the action, for example, in the selfishness of the characters, in the novel's pessimism and determinism, and in the suggestion that only through the disinterested contemplation of art can life's problems be transcended.

More generally, one can see in the wide scope and the social concerns of *The Princess Casamassima* evidence of James's attempt to imitate popular novelists like Eliot, Thackeray, Balzac, and Zola. Whether or not it is accurate to call *The Princess Casamassima* a "naturalistic" novel depends primarily upon what one means by this elusive term. Certainly ingredients such as the following suggest links to *L'Assommoir* and *Germinal*: James's stress on the importance of Hyacinth's heredity, and the way in which his environment acts on his inherited character; the novelist's original inclination to work up his subject by visiting Millbank Prison clutching his notebook; his willingness to deal with a class of characters lower than his norm; and his use of a highly intrusive narrator throughout the novel. On the other hand, James's pointed references in his preface to the intelligence and sensitivity of his central character, the ironic contrast he draws there between a literal kind of notetaking and the "notes" of the "preoccupied painter with a penetrating imagination" (1:xxii), his avoidance of the overtly sexual, and his seemingly deliberate suppression of specific descriptions of the really ugly, dirty, or shockingly sensational, all suggest a conscious effort to distinguish his novel from other examples of the genre.

A reader interested in sources must also consider the relationship between this novel and James's own experiences (other than those of walking the London streets), as well as between *The Princess Casamassima* and James's earlier fiction. Certainly the frustration that he revealed in letters over problems not being dealt with influenced the novel, as did his sense that he was living in a disintegrating culture. With regard to his awareness of radical political and social organizations, the consensus is that he was reasonably knowledgeable, in part because of his family background (his father had several friends who supported Fourier), his reading (newspapers, nonfiction), and his friendships with people like Turgenev (who knew the anarchist Prince Kropotkin) and the *Nation* editor E. L. Godkin, who were themselves interested in political issues.

Several critics have also speculated about possible nonliterary sources of characters in the novel, the consensus being that there are obvious (if probably unconscious) parallels between Rosy Muniment and James's sister Alice, and between Paul Muniment and William James; the ambiguous friendship between the cool revolutionary and Hyacinth Robinson may be an unconscious mirroring of the relation between the two James brothers. A few critics have wondered about James's inspiration for the Princess; there is no consensus here, but it seems likely that he either knew personally or knew about a woman (or women) who either suggested to him Christina's fascinating and explosive combination of qualities, or made him confident that a character whom he had already imagined did actually exist.

Christina is the only major character in James's fiction whom he was willing to treat again, primarily, as he suggests in his preface, because there remained from *Roderick Hudson* unexplored dimensions of her personality. A probable additional reason for his interest (and his decision to name his novel after her) was his desire to increase his novel's chances of success, because James knew before he began to serialize that the serialization of *The Bostonians* was not being well received. The reappearances of Christina, Madame Grandioni, and the Prince have encouraged some critics to see in *Roderick Hudson* an important "source" for *The Princess Casamassima,* in particular for James's conception of the Princess's motives in immersing herself in radical politics—a desire to expiate her guilt for allowing herself to be forced into a barren marriage, for example.

An important dimension of *The Princess Casamassima* is the search of both Hyacinth and Christina for a stable and fulfilling identity, a quest that is crucial to, for example, Christopher Newman (*The American*), Isabel Archer (*The Portrait of a Lady*), and Verena Tarrant (*The Bostonians*). One can also see in *The Princess Casamassima* evidence of James's continuing fascination with the relationship between innocence and experience, poles that he most frequently identified with the American as opposed to the European (or Europeanized American) points of view. It is the appearance of this theme in *The Princess* that has caused Ferner Nuhn to suggest that there are closer links between James's so-called international novels and this one than there might initially seem to be.

James in his preface points to a formal link between this novel and his earlier ones—in his preference for seeing the action through the eyes of an intelligent, sensitive, but at times bewildered observer—a person who is at once a character and a means by which the reader can be given a "felt impression" of the action. Rowland Mallet (*Roderick Hudson*) is an obvious analogue to Hyacinth Robinson here, but so too, in part, are Christopher Newman, Isabel Archer, and Basil Ransom (*The Bostonians*), not to mention the multifarious observer-participants in James's short fiction, or even in his travel writings.[7] James's somewhat uneasy preference in this novel for the wonders of individual relations and the marvels of culture over the concern for social issues is also a common response in much of his fiction. Another interest linking this novel to the earlier fiction is what might be called "woman's role," the reference to Schopenhauer symbolizing the biases against which women struggle. That James was not overly sympathetic to the more flamboyant manifestations of the nineteenth-century women's movement is obvious from *The Bostonians*; yet his interest is also obvious in much of what he wrote prior to *The Princess Casamassima.*

Are all of these ideas, themes, conceptions, relationships "sources" for the novel? It is hard to say. Richard Gill has argued that James's treatment of Gardencourt in *Portrait,* and the influence of this magnificent house on Isabel's character, is an obvious source for his treatment of Medley in the later novel. A source also is the confidence evinced by James in his 1884 "Art of Fiction" article in the ability of someone "upon whom nothing is lost" to guess the "unseen from the seen"; this feeling may be a "source" for his decision in *Princess* to eschew the technique of literal note-taking and to depend upon his own fragmentary knowledge for the novel's portrayal of radical activity and the real plight of the poor. All these factors—James's reading, his response to the London environment, his imagination, his family and acquaintances, his own books—had some influence on *The Princess Casamassima*. Although it is impossible to decide to what extent each of these factors contributed to the creation of the novel, its origins were considerably more complex than the pattern of composition traced in James's somewhat misleading preface.

Radicalism in *The Princess Casamassima*

Most criticism written about *The Princess Casamassima* has focused on one of a small list of interrelated topics: the motivation of the Princess, the suicide of Hyacinth Robinson, and the quality of the work as a sociopolitical novel. Many critics have recognized the importance of the last topic because of its relevance to *The Princess Casamassima* and to James's reputation as a whole. Since James began to publish major fiction, he has provoked both discerning admiration and well-informed hostility: there seems always to have been "the question of Henry James," an important and controversial part of which has centered on his ostensibly limited emotional and thematic range. Readers of our own era who observe in James's massive post–1950 critical reputation a vivid example of the emperor's new clothes are sometimes appalled by the implied inclusion of this coterie novelist in the company of giants like Balzac, Dickens, Eliot, Tolstoy, and Faulkner. On the other hand, readers who admire James and applaud his reputation will sometimes acknowledge his narrowness while stressing his depth—the wonder of his achievements within a limited scope. Other defenders will point to the supposed excellence of a novel like *The Princess Casamassima* as an example of what James could create, and perhaps could have continued to write, if circumstances and his own natural inclinations had not led him in different directions.

A common complaint of recent critics is that the novel unfairly trivializes radical activity: nowhere, they argue, is there one radical or sympathizer with the poor whose desire to ameliorate social conditions does not derive from essentially selfish, delusive, even pathological motives; everywhere radicalism is handled with contempt (as in James's treatment of the malcontents at the Sun and Moon) or somewhat amused condescension (as in the Princess's characterization).

In defence of James, it should be pointed out that the novel does not exclude the possibility of partially disinterested motivation. Coexisting, for example, with Paul Muniment's desire for revenge against the social system that has helped destroy his parents, with his attempt to aggrandize himself and his exasperating sister, and with his loathing for the "unclean beasts" (1:352) whom he wants to rise above, is a genuine belief that "The low tone of our fellow mortals is a result of bad conditions" (2:216), and that "present arrangements won't do. They won't do" (2:217). There is evidence also that not all of Christina's reasons for wanting to embrace radical activity are selfish. At times, of course, a drive to escape boredom, part of which is sexual, energizes the Princess; or a desire to expiate her marriage in *Roderick Hudson* to the Prince—an act that Madame Grandioni calls half-ironically a "horrible piece of frivolity" (1:307); or to escape the frustration of being a merely decorative female in a culture where crucial actions are performed by males. These essentially environmental factors combine with her innate capriciousness and love of the histrionic to explain most of Christina's actions. Yet James suggests that her activity may be in "good faith" (2:174): part of her personality sympathizes with the poor and probably cares about individuals like Hyacinth, as is implied at the end of the novel in her concern for the young bookbinder (even though one motive is to seize the heroic "masculine" role of assassin for herself). Moreover, her hatred of the upper class at times seems passionately sincere—in the following outburst to Lady Aurora, for example: "Haven't you judged it like me, condemned it and given it up? Aren't you sick of the egotism, the snobbery, the meanness, the frivolity, the immorality, the hypocrisy?" (2:199).

It should be observed also that nothing definite is known about the motives of two other radicals, Schinkel and the leader, Hoffendahl. Some readers have felt that in his handling of Hyacinth's dilemma near the end of the novel, James intends to suggest something quite negative about the callousness of radical groups—their treatment of persons as pawns or abstractions, thus (to quote the narrator about the Princess), raising themselves "straight out of the bad air of the personal" (2:406). Rather than observing implied criticism, however, one might speak of the author's objectivity, his dispassionate awareness that revolutionaries of all kinds need, at times, to shut off parts of themselves in order to maintain their radical identities. As Paul Muniment says in a "low and grave" manner to the Princess in response to her plea to save Hyacinth: "But you ought to remember that in the line you've chosen our affections, our natural ties, our timidities, our shrinkings. . . . All those things are as nothing, they must never weigh a feather, beside our service" (2:299). There is none of the irony here that typifies James's treatment of pronouncements by the radicals; this statement has dignity and power. Yet, even after observing examples of James's ostensible attempt to balance the prevailing skepticism of the novel, one may conclude that the attempt seems halfhearted. And readers who yearn for the presence of at least one unequivocally humane, well-balanced, and dedicated revolutionary must remain disappointed by this dimension of *The Princess Casamassima.*

Poverty and Wealth in the Novel

Such readers are likely to be (and have been) even more disappointed by James's general treatment of poverty—those conditions that radical activity is designed to alleviate. This is not to suggest James lacked awareness of the issues about London's poor that many social activists were discovering and becoming involved in during the latter part of the nineteenth century. The most memorable evidence of this awareness is the powerful scene set in the ugly and terrifying Millbank Prison—the eventual fate of many of the poor. Occasional references also call the reader's attention to the living conditions of some poor people: the area around Audley Court, for example, where, to Hyacinth, "everything that covered the earth was ugly and sordid and seemed to express or to represent the weariness of toil" (1:243); and Lomax Place itself, which, after Hyacinth returns from Medley, "was pitiful to the verge of sickening." There is also the reference to "the most fetid holes in London" (2:260) where Hyacinth apparently leads the Princess during her quixotic quests for the squalid. Other brief, occasional references point to the problems of lack of work (2:339, 344), dearth of food (2:168), large families (1:124), and the "hard dreary problems of misery and crime" (2:196).

Despite references like these, however, James's novel as a whole provokes little sympathy for the poor, in part because the book contains few detailed, particular dramatizations of their problems. Late in the novel, for example, several allusions are made to the visits of Hyacinth and the Princess to the worst sections of London—scenes apparently of "unspeakable misery and horror" (2:243), the "darkest places" (2:260), a "sea of barbarism" (2:262). And, early in the novel, reference is made to the family of Millicent Henning having plunged to "the very bottom" after fleeing Lomax Place (1:66). Each reference is so vague as to be almost meaningless.

At one point Hyacinth in thinking about Lady Aurora concludes that "the rich couldn't consider poverty in the light of experience. Their mistakes and illusions, their thinking they had got hold of the sensations of want and dirt when they hadn't at all, would always be more or less irritating" (1:316). Observing this, a reader might conclude that James's reluctance to describe scenes of poverty is based upon tact and respect for the uniqueness of the poor's experience; yet at times James is more than willing to be powerfully picturesque in reporting Hyacinth's responses to the dirtiness of poor people, for example, "There were nights when everyone he met appeared to reek with gin and filth and he found himself elbowed by figures as foul as lepers. Some of the women and girls in particular were appalling—saturated with alcohol and vice, brutal, bedraggled, obscene" (2:267).

A major conclusion to be drawn from the vagueness of the references to the conditions of the poor and the vehemence of the statements condemning poor people is that James, like his point-of-view character, is most frequently struck, not by the potential value of efforts to ameliorate the environment of poverty, but instead by the poor's "brutal insensibility, a grossness of proof against the taste of better things and against any desire for them" (2:262). Moreover, other aspects of James's treatment of the problems of the poor suggest his almost temperamental unwillingness to take these problems seriously or to regard them with as much sympathy and respect as they deserve. The potential force of references mentioned earlier relating to people out of work, for example, is mostly dissipated because such references are made by habitués of the Sun and Moon, almost all of whom James treats negatively. Moreover, information that another novelist might have used to provoke sympathy for the poor James often used for different purposes. One notes, for example, the condescending comedy in the following reference to the pupils at a school which Hyacinth had attended as a child: "such pupils as could be spared (in their families) from the more urgent exercise of holding the baby and fetching the beer" (1:100).

Another dimension of *The Princess Casamassima* that irritates or angers some readers is James's periodic practice of inviting more sympathy for members of the upper class than the lower. An obvious case in point is the sympathy Hyacinth comes to feel for the Prince as both of them observe Paul Muniment entering the house of the Princess: " 'Is *that* for the revolution?' the trembling nobleman panted. But Mr. Robinson made no answer; he only gazed at the closed door an instant and then, disengaging himself, walked straight away, leaving the victim of the wrong he could even then feel as deeper than his own to shake, in the dark, a helpless foolish gold-headed stick at the indifferent house" (2:324). An analogy to this kind of scene is Zola's treatment in *Germinal* of a mine manager, M. Hennebeau, who, sexually humiliated by his imperious wife (who is sleeping with his nephew), concludes: "He would have given everything, his education, his comfort, his luxury, his power as manager, if he could be for one day the last of the wretches who obeyed him, free of his flesh, enough of a blackguard to beat his wife and to take his pleasure with his neighbours' wives. And he longed also to be dying of hunger, to have an empty belly, a stomach twisted by cramps that would make his head turn with giddiness: perhaps that would have killed the eternal pain."[8]

The contrast is significant, however, between the effects that James and Zola achieve through their treatments of the suffering cuckolded husbands. Although in *Germinal* the reader knows that, at this particular moment, the anguished upper-middle-class man is sincere and his pain is excruciating, the reader also has observed enough detailed depictions of poverty in the novel to realize that, relatively speaking, the man's problems are picayune, and that he does not know what he is wishing upon himself. The seemingly desired effect in James's novel, on the other hand, is to push the reader to conclude that all people have their problems, which are not necessarily tied to social class or economic status.

A final symptomatic example of James's handling of details related to the conditions of poverty is the following description, which appears during the scene when the healthy and vigorous Millicent Henning reappears in Lomax Place after an absence of many years. As her eyes wander around Pinnie's quarters, Millicent "noticed that though it was already November there was no fire in the neatly-kept grate beneath the chimney-piece, on which a design, partly architectural, partly botanical, executed in the hair of Miss Pynsent's parents, was flanked by a pair of vases, under glass, containing muslin flowers" (1:62). What happens in this description is that, having observed from Milly's perspective a certain type of privation (lack of heat), the narrator passes quickly on to details of at least equal interest to him—evidence suggesting Pinnie's vulgar taste. Even if one chooses to argue that, in focusing on the design, James does not intend mild satire at Pinnie's expense but is merely being "objective" in naturalist fashion, one must grant nonetheless that an effect of this technique of the rapidly moving camera is to encourage the reader to skim over the details about the lack of fire. In a novel purporting to deal in a nontrivial way with conditions of English poverty, we might argue legitimately that such details should be highlighted, not submerged.

The Treatment of Hyacinth Robinson

Early in this discussion the scene in Millbank Prison was used as evidence of James's awareness of problems endemic to the poor. It is doubtful, however, that the primary effect of the scene is to raise our awareness of the difficulties of the poor in general: for most readers, the scene points to a major source of Hyacinth Robinson's particular identity problems. One might argue, of course, that because Hyacinth is himself a representative figure, any factor helping to explain the development of his personality and existential predicament will also reflect on the plight of the poor. As the widely disparate critical responses to Hyacinth suggest, however, the question of his putative representativeness is highly debatable.

Critics impressed by James's handling of the novel's social themes tend to praise him for his willingness to imagine a lower-class person with tastes and capabilities similar to his own—a kind of mute inglorious Henry James. For such critics, the links between Hyacinth and his creator—which James refers to in the preface—evince the author's catholic sympathies and ultimately democratic faith in the potentiality of common people. According to Paul Dolan, the same qualities are revealed in the parallel suggested between Hyacinth and Hamlet. The problem with these arguments is that, for many readers, the links between Hyacinth and James or Hamlet—even Hyacinth and John Keats—are not felt to reflect upon the value of the poor in general. Instead, such parallels suggest what the rest of the novel seems intent on conveying: that Hyacinth is a very special case. F. W. Dupee (a strong admirer of James) refers to Hyacinth as "James's sensibilities cast for a time among thieves but instructed to come home at last, immaculate as ever although with a bullet through the heart." Other critics hostile to James, such as Maxwell Geismar, observe in the links between Hyacinth and James evidence of the author's fatuous and deluding narcissism.

Even if we reject the inimical notion that, through Hyacinth, James was playing out a subconscious masochistic fable about his own lack of popularity and/or failure to penetrate the English upper class, we still may not regard Hyacinth as a representative figure, and may discern difficulties in James's method of relating Hyacinth to the more general areas of radicalism and poverty. Twice the narrator speaks of Hyacinth as a representative of his class. Early we are told that, despite his "exotic" quality, "yet, with his sharp young face, destitute of bloom but not of sweetness, and a certain conscious cockneyism that pervaded him, he was as strikingly as Millicent, in her own degree, a product of the London streets and the London air" (1:79). Later, when Hyacinth visits the Princess for the first time, we are told how he is "stamped with that extraordinary transformation which the British Sunday often operates in the person of the wage-earning cockney" (1:280). Yet because of the way in which Hyacinth is treated during much of the novel, many readers will experience him only as an individual with highly unusual qualities, living in an idiosyncratic situation.

Evidence is everywhere of Hyacinth's special nature—his intense general susceptibility to environmental stimuli and his particular hatred of dirt and ugliness, and love of the most delicately beautiful impressions. The individual manifestations of Hyacinth's general propensity seem inherited (although cultivated also by the relatively fastidious Pinnie and Vetch). Because so much is made of Hyacinth's probable father, Lord Frederick, we assume that the qualities have something to do with the aristocracy, and since Hyacinth's French ancestry is so often stressed, they also seem related to race. In any event, they have little to do with the English poor. Additional evidence of Hyacinth's special—what might be called "artistic"—nature may be found in the way in which he responds to contrasting environments in two crucial, contiguous scenes: one focuses on the Sun and Moon and culminates in Hyacinth's vow and midnight visit to Hoffendahl; in the other, we abruptly awaken with Hyacinth at Medley, the country house rented by the Princess from unnamed impecunious aristocrats.

Everything in the first environment suggests a loathsome charade as dirty, self-indulgent men put on radical faces to meet other radical faces. Near the end, the "supposititious hairdresser," Mr. Delancey, cries out self-importantly: "There isn't a man in the blessed lot of you that isn't afraid of his bloody skin—afraid, afraid, afraid!"; this accusation "affected Hyacinth like a quick blow in the face: it seemed to leap at him personally, as if a three-legged stool or some hideous hobnailed boot had been shied at him" (1:359). The intensity of Hyacinth's response and the fact he is driven by it to leap on to a chair to defend his sincerity and make his vow all suggest that the scene and the challenge have touched something deep in the young man's psyche. The reader senses here that Hyacinth must act now or lose his faith in everything, most crucially the possibility of a radical self. It could be argued, in fact, that the vow (which smacks ironically of the "gentleman") really gives birth to this self. Yet the birth seems cesarean—a self painfully forced out of Hyacinth by frustration and disgust.

On the other hand, it is abundantly clear that the environment at Medley is natural to Hyacinth, despite his self-consciousness. He unequivocally belongs. All the impressions he soaks in as he wanders through this dreamworld suggest a melding of his essential self with it. His subsequent experiences in Paris and Venice only confirm one's conviction that Hyacinth should be cocooned in beautiful worlds, particularly those that stimulate the visual sense. Ironically, of course, after he returns to London his special sensibility and his highly unusual circumstances combine to alienate him from the world in which he is compelled to live. As the novel proceeds, several characters inflict on Hyacinth some variation of the phrases "bloated little swell" (2:216) or "duke in disguise" (2:217), and although the source of Hyacinth's sensibility remains ambiguous, it seems unrelated to the English lower class.

Thus, although through Hyacinth we learn much about someone who loses access to tastes most easily indulged in affluent surroundings, we learn little about what it is like to be physically poor. We learn about someone who is denied "French Cookery" (2:170) but who does not lack food; and about a person appalled by the ugliness of his work environment but who does not lack work. A key scene with Paul Muniment asks the reader to sympathize with Hyacinth's "rather helpless sense that, whatever he saw, he saw—and this was always the case—so many other things besides. He saw the immeasurable misery of the people, and yet he saw all that had been, as it were, rescued and redeemed from it" (2:217). Many readers may legitimately doubt Hyacinth's insight into the "immeasurable misery of the people."

Related to this conclusion is the contention of several critics that Hyacinth is a "prig" and a "snob" and that James either does not recognize these qualities or supports them. There is evidence both to justify the use of such labels and to suggest that James is aware of these qualities in his hero. There is evidence also that James was worried (understandably, given the reader complaints about the coldness of *The Bostonians*) about the willingness of his audience to care about his theme and characters: early in the novel, Mr. Vetch cries in frustration: "What does it matter after all, and why do you worry? What difference can it make what happens—on either side—to such low people?"

(1:39). James tries to make his story "matter" to his readers by keeping
under careful control his own tendency to be amused at some actions
of his adolescent protagonist, even when these might warrant a more
satirical treatment. What is being suggested here is that, often, James
sees through Hyacinth's ridiculous self-consciousness and fastidiousness; at the same time, in trying to maintain reader sympathy for the
"little hero," James chooses to downplay the young man's occasional
asininity—so much so, in fact, that readers may not notice the ridi-
cule. Typically, James attempts to create his delicate balance by having
the narrator plead for sympathy on the character's behalf or having
Hyacinth recognize his own silliness.

An example of James's technique is his handling of Hyacinth's trip
to the theater with Milly to view *The Pearl of Paraguay,* during which
he is introduced to the Princess. Of the mob scene in front of the
theater where Hyacinth thinks about a possible row and ways in which
he might "distinguish himself," the narrator writes, "he scarcely knew
in what way and imagined himself more easily routing some hulking
adversary by an exquisite application of the retort courteous than by
flying at him with a pair of very small fists" (1:187–88). The Hyacinth
described here combines self-consciousness, priggishness, a potent
need to express himself in stereotypically masculine ways, and rueful
awareness of the difficulty he will have in doing this. The tone mixes
wry humor with sympathy.

At one point during the subsequent scene (or "occasion," the term
sometimes used by James in his prefaces to refer to these lengthy sequences told through a combination of dialogue and narrative commentary), the narrator refers to Hyacinth's "easily-excited organism"
(1:192); throughout, the reader is allowed to experience the meaning
of this phrase. Around the middle, when Hyacinth is about to meet
the Princess, he feels "that he himself ought perhaps to resent the idea
of being served up for the entertainment of capricious not to say pre-
sumptuous triflers, but that somehow he didn't, and that it was more
worthy of the part he aspired to play in life to meet such occasions
calmly and urbanely than to take the trouble of avoidance" (1:200).
James's comic sense of his hero's posturing is clearly in evidence, as it
is later when he encounters the divine Christina. One's sympathy for
him is maintained throughout, however, in part because we observe
most of the action from his perspective (despite occasional ironic or
sympathetic asides from the narrator), but also because of Hyacinth's
own befuddled quasi-insights into his helplessness and ridiculousness:

"how could he know moreover what was natural to a person in that exaltation of grace and splendor? Perhaps it was her habit to send out every evening for some witless stranger to amuse her; perhaps that was the way the foreign aristocracy lived" (1:212).

A final example of James's complex handling of his protagonist is related to the lengthy passage from Hyacinth's Venetian letter to the Princess in which he expatiates about "The Venetian girl-face," the beauty of "the shuffling clicking maidens who work in the bead-factories," and the "degradation" of English women who "wear the hideous British bonnet" (2:142–3). The reader observes how Hyacinth skims over details about these "underfed" Italian maidens that might have provoked sociopolitical comment, and instead lingers over pleasing aesthetic impressions. That James was conscious of Hyacinth's principle of selection is suggested not only by the irony in language such as "degradation" but also by Hyacinth's guilt upon returning to his job: "What struck him most . . . was the simple synthetic patience of the others who had bent *their* backs and felt the rub of that dirty drapery while he was lounging in the halls of Medley, dawdling through boulevards and museums and admiring the purity of the Venetian girl-face" (2:157). One dimension of Hyacinth that emerges as the novel proceeds is the person who sees in Paris primarily "a civilization that had no visible rough spots" (2:121) and who is disconcerted when Lady Aurora loses interest in "the Ruskinian theories of Venice" and "his views of some of the arrière-pensées of M. Gambetta . . . not altogether, as he thought, deficient in originality" (2:191). James sympathizes with and respects his hero; he also seems willing to laugh at Hyacinth's special sensibility, which in some ways is so much like his own.

Hyacinth's Suicide

Most discussions of the novel have speculated about the reasons for Hyacinth's suicide or its possible relation to the sociopolitical themes. Both are difficult to determine. By the time Hyacinth decides to visit Millicent at her shop, he is horribly confused; yet he still considers performing the assassination, as he has throughout book 6, despite his "horror of the public reappearance, in his person, of the imbrued hands of his mother" (2:419). Several reasons are suggested for this leaning toward violence, one of which is that he has not given up completely on the cause: although he is not convinced that the assassination will "clearly help" (2:404), he also cannot be certain that it will not. Another important reason is his desire not to provide evidence for those (perhaps even himself) who suspect him of being merely ornamental and incapable of this kind of action. Because he respects Paul Muniment, Hyacinth is particularly bothered by Paul's consistently belittling remarks, and he wants to prove that Paul is wrong. Related to this and probably the most important reason—ironically—derives from Hyacinth's desired image of himself as a gentleman. There are several suggestions made during the novel that Hyacinth is infatuated with an aristocratic male code, in part derived from his reading but also related, it is implied, to his subconscious fears about his masculinity. Told by Schinkel that the Poupins "think it no disgrace if you've changed," Hyacinth replies, "That's very well for her; but it's pitiful for him" (2:376). Later he says, "Lord, how shaky you all are!" and the narrator writes, "He was more and more aware now of the superiority still left him to cling to" (2:377). A sign of superiority is the willingness to honor a vow, in this case to assassinate a member of the aristocracy, a possible course of action that Hyacinth never rejects totally.

At the same time, many other factors pressure him to act differently: the countervow to Vetch made, by Pinnie's memory, that "I shall never do any of their work" (2:391) (Hyacinth may be lying here, since we are told at the beginning of his "intense determination to dissemble before his visitor to the last" (2:387); his conviction that he is no longer important to either Paul or the Princess ("He was overpast, he had become vague, he was extinct" [2:418]); and in particular his feeling that violence would act as a posthumous insult to his mother (2:419).

It is important to point out here that, although a great deal has been made by some critics about how Hyacinth's suicide is a noble sacrifice on behalf of Arnoldian high culture, during the last book of the novel this theme is not emphasized. Certainly we have been told earlier about the importance of beauty to Hyacinth and about his fear of artistic achievements being desecrated in a revolution; yet this motive is not reintroduced, except by implication. In fact, when at the end Hyacinth wanders through London before deciding to visit Millicent's haberdashery, the image of culture that dominates his mind is not primarily of marvellous impressions (although these are present) but imperviousness: "He . . . looked up at the huge fretted palace that rose there as a fortress of the social order which he, like the young David, had been commissioned to attack with a sling and pebble" (2:420).

At this point in his wandering, when he decides to visit Millicent,

Hyacinth is almost exhausted: he has not slept well for several days and has awakened this morning "at the earliest dawn" (2:418). Moreover, the pressures that tear him in opposite directions are so potent that, despite his pride, "a vision rose before him of a quick flight with her, for an undefined purpose, to an undefined spot" (2:421). Characteristically, however, his reaction to this unmanly possibility is to blush. Then he rationalizes: "Again and again, all the same, he indulged in the reflection that spontaneous uncultivated minds often have inventions, inspirations." This is followed by a final exhilarating thought: "he might at least feel the firm roundness of her arms about him. He didn't exactly know what good this would do him or what door it would open, but he should like it" (2:421). Significantly, this possibility is sexual (although there is also a suggestion of his need to be mothered).

As Hyacinth prepares to seek Millicent, "he hovered a long time, undecided, embarrassed, half-ashamed"; then, upon entering the store, he walks "as if he had as good a right as anyone else" (2:422). Both responses strongly suggest his continual insecurity and lack of self-confidence. Since these qualities are combined with the young man's "sore personal need" of Millicent, it is easy to understand why his discovery of Captain Sholto, "with his eyes travelling up and down the front of their beautiful friend's person" (2:423), is so devastating. James is characteristically coy about what the eyes of the two men "said to each other" when they meet over Millicent's shoulder, but we may guess the message which Hyacinth deciphers: that, again, he has been "superseded indeed" (2:399).

In the light of all the pressures on Hyacinth and the shock of this last encounter, the only thing mildly surprising about his suicide is that it takes him so long to perform the act: Hyacinth's visit to the shop takes place during the day (perhaps as early as the morning), the Princess arrives at his room "about nine o'clock" (2:423), and Schinkel assumes that Hyacinth shoots himself when the landlady is out "fetching the milk" (2:430), about a half hour before Christina's arrival. We do not know why Hyacinth waits as long as he does because, during these hours, we are denied access to his thoughts. As with the suicide itself, however, James's method encourages readers to draw their own conclusions. Perhaps, as Hyacinth has tried to do throughout, he fights against the part of his personality attracted to death and roams London seeking a way out or waits in his room hoping, consciously or unconsciously, for a friend to invade his loneliness. Perhaps he delays out of

fear and fastidiousness and shoots himself only after the confusion created by the coming of night—we have been told earlier that night is
the worst time for Hyacinth—is too much to endure.

Whatever the motive, the time lapse suggests a clinging to life until
the last moment; it further suggests that, had the Princess come earlier, Hyacinth might not have committed suicide that evening. On the
other hand, suicide seems the only real option available to the young
man. If he chooses either to perform the assassination or to avoid it,
he is likely to be killed by the state or the enemies of it; and in making
either choice he painfully and deeply violates an essential part of his
being. Hyacinth is thus imprisoned by both circumstances and self.
Whether we interpret the suicide as an act of despair or heroism depends upon our own values and the way in which we understand Hyacinth's state of mind just prior to death. In any event, through the
suicide, Hyacinth escapes from prison.

Critics who observe in Hyacinth Robinson the sensitivity of the art-
ist-aesthete sometimes argue that *The Princess Casamassima* is not
"really" about revolution, radical activity, or poverty, at all. A conclusion like this is simplistic, and not merely because so many characters
other than the hero reflect upon these themes. Hyacinth himself is the
best example of a tendency that James observes in most characters: to
identify for egotistical reasons with organizations devoted to social
causes. Moreover, Hyacinth's eventual skepticism about the selfish motives of radicals and his fear of the results of their actions—that Hoffendahl "would cut up the ceilings of the Veronese into strips, so that
everyone might have a little piece" (2:353)—relate directly to the political theme, whether or not we agree with these feelings. Relevant
also is Hyacinth's admiration for those classic works of art whose creation may depend upon the existence of the very class system which
his friends want to destroy. And Hyacinth's suicide is relevant, too,
although the political causes are tied up with other factors such as his
search for an identity and his friendship with Paul Muniment. The
novel, then, is very much involved with sociopolitical concerns, even
though in ways that may seem incomplete or trivializing or unrealistic
to many readers.

Chapter Three

The Tragic Muse:
James's Neglected Novel

Background

Genesis and text. James dispatched the last installment of *The Princess Casamassima* to the *Atlantic* in early July 1886 and then finished reading proofs for the book publication in late October. Writing to his brother on 10 September just after returning from a brief working holiday with some artist friends (one of whom was John Sargent), James spoke of his desire "to do some short things—half a dozen little critical papers among them. The next novels I do are to be but half as long as these two last, and I never again mean to do anything nearly so long as the Princess."[1] During the next extremely productive year and a half, he wrote literary criticism (resulting in the 1888 publication of *Partial Portraits*), some of his most skillful short fiction (including "The Aspern Papers"), and the international novella *The Reverberator.* Part of the time, beginning in early December 1886, was spent in Italy, particularly in Florence, where he saw a great deal of his admirer, the American author Constance Fenimore Woolson; during the remaining period, beginning in late July, he resided primarily at De Vere Gardens.

Upon his return to England James had already begun to think about *The Tragic Muse,* which he assumed would not be serialized. By early March, however, James committed himself to a long serial for the *Atlantic Monthly,* the opening chapters for which he was confident he could provide by October. After working on the serial for over a year (its seventeen installments ran from January 1889 to May 1890), he completed revisions for the book version by the spring of 1890. One thousand copies of the two-volume American edition were published by Houghton, Mifflin in June 1890, and five hundred copies of the three-volume English edition were published by Macmillan in the same month. A second English one-volume edition of two thousand copies was published in early 1891.[2] And a revised version was prepared by James for his New York Edition (vol. 7–8, 1908).

Following his usual practice, James did not make extensive revisions for the first book edition, contenting himself almost exclusively with eliminating commas and creating contractions. One name was changed: the politician-painter Nick Dormer's first riding was changed from Crackhurst to the slightly more euphonious Crockhurst, James seemingly believing that one ugly name (Harsh) would suggest the aesthetically unpleasant nature of Nick's political involvement. On the other hand, James revised extensively for the New York Edition, eliminating contractions, making many changes in word choice—sometimes eliminating words so as to tighten sentences, often adding words so as to make the novel more theatrical (by enabling readers to visualize scenes more easily or imagine tones of voices, for example); moreover, some revisions clarify character motivation or illuminate relationships.

Another revision made by James was to divide the fifty-one-chapter novel into eight "books," a practice he had not followed with the revisions of *Roderick Hudson, The American,* or *The Portrait of a Lady,* but which he began when he revised *The Princess Casamassima.* Although there is not space here to discuss fully the effects that a novelist may create through this type of closure, it is important to suggest that such effects are often not trivial. The pauses forced by the technique, for example, among other things emphasize the importance of certain sections for the reader, invite him to ponder the implications of what he has read before rushing toward the next plot development, and encourage him to discern relationships between structural elements that the "book" designation has called attention to. To be more specific, a reader experiences *The Tragic Muse* differently because of the "books" division than he does if he reads it in serial, or, in one of the earlier editions where the chapters are interrupted somewhat arbitrarily by volume endings imposed primarily by the publisher, not the author. Certainly part of the experience provoked by the 1908 division is aesthetic pleasure: one senses a conscious, complex, interesting narrative control. The impression that may be created by the earlier texts, on the other hand, is of a very long, almost undifferentiated narrative stream. Readers who search for structure may receive a contrasting, but equally unflattering impression: of a novel organized according to a mechanical principle of simple alternation between the plot involving Nick Dormer and the one centering on the diplomat Peter Sherringham. A reader's sense, in the revised text, of a more complex ordering within a simple binary pattern is a fairer and more generous response to the novel James has written.

Source and influence. Although James said in letters and *Note-books* entries while writing the novel that he had not relinquished his plan of eventually devoting himself to short fiction on the models of Ivan Turgenev and Guy de Maupassant, his fears about cash flow dissuaded him from depending upon the medium at this time as his sole source of income. Thus, a prime reason for beginning *The Tragic Muse*—despite the possible pressure, boredom, and exhaustion connected with this lengthy serial—was James's felt need for cash.

This is not to suggest that money was the only motivation or that James loathed the activity. Comments made while he was writing the serial, in fact, suggest his enjoyment and pride in the novel. The general conflict between art and the world had fascinated him for many years. Other facets of the novel he also was interested in and knew intimately—the milieu of the aesthete, for example, which was useful both as an object of satire and a means to satirize English philistinism. Moreover, he had loved the world of the theater since childhood; later he was a constant playgoer, he knew actresses and knew about acting, and he always welcomed the chance to criticize the low standards of the English stage. Also, he had read fiction about the theater, and, with typical competitiveness, was confident that he could do better.[3]

In addition, his knowledge of the visual arts was extensive, and he had several artist friends. Moreover, the vicissitudes of John Sargent's career had made James aware of how difficult it was to be a portrait painter who was talented and successful—a problem analogous to that of a novelist like himself. Politics and diplomacy would have to be included, of course, but James was familiar with these worlds, although not fascinated by them; also, a minute analysis of contemporary issues like Home Rule for Ireland would be unnecessary. In sum, James was in better control of his material before beginning *The Tragic Muse* than he had been before *The Bostonians* or *The Princess*. As well, his use of quasi-naturalistic ideas and techniques in those novels helped prepare him to deal with the compositional challenges presented by this new work.

There is another crucial source of *The Tragic Muse*—James's interest in the theme of vocation, one central to many of Gabriel Nash's monologues and to the lives of the novel's major characters. Several of James's tales and novels written during this period touched upon this theme—"The Author of Beltraffio" and "The Lesson of the Master," for

example, and *The Bostonians* and *The Princess*—particularly as a problem
of individual vocation related to marriage. Although, as Kenneth Graham has argued eloquently, James's interest in vocation was present
from the beginning of his career, several factors may have made his
interest unusually acute during these years: the death of his father,
whose theories are often echoed by Gabriel Nash; the tragic spectacle
of Alice James, whose vocation seemed to be illness; the incipient success of William James, who had found a vocation after a long, anguished search; Henry's own thoughts about a change of artistic
direction—perhaps even his ruminations about the ways in which marriage might have affected—or might affect—his career. Several years
earlier, James had decided not to marry, his conscious reason being
that marriage would harm his career. Yet Leon Edel's fascinating account of James's friendship during these years with the American novelist Constance Fenimore Woolson invites speculation that he may have
begun to waver in his resolve. Moreover, as Ross Posnock's recently
published book suggests, Robert Browning—who had become James's
neighbor in De Vere Gardens—"sacrificed nothing; indeed he enjoyed
the luxury of a rich personal life and a fertile creative existence. . . .
Browning, in effect, exposes James's version of Balzac [that art is 'ruin-
ously expensive'] to be an elaborate fiction that rationalized James's
retreat from the demands of the 'sacred relation' between men and
women." Whatever the specific reasons, James's fascination with the
problem of vocation pervades *The Tragic Muse.*

In Defense of *The Tragic Muse*

Although James's intention when he began to write *The Tragic Muse*
was to make it only half as long as *The Princess Casamassima,* it is,
ironically, his longest serialized novel. In all probability it is also the
novel by him least often read and least highly regarded, despite the
occasionally brilliant critical attempts to create an audience for it, and
despite James's own generally positive attitude toward the novel.[4] A
major reason *The Tragic Muse* does not provoke the sympathetic response it deserves is that it is in significant ways different from the
more critically acclaimed fiction that precedes and follows it. The novel
lacks, for example, the at times cruelly satiric point of view, late nineteenth-century topicality, and touch of abnormal psychology of *The
Bostonians.* It lacks, as well, the tragic dimension of *The Princess Casamassima* and a dominating center of consciousness. Moreover, it fails to

provide critics with the challenge to epistemological and ethical deconstruction inspired by such fiction as *The Spoils of Poynton, The Turn of the Screw,* and *The Sacred Fount.* Also, in its more or less old-fashioned handling of narrative point of view and dramatic scene it is less technically experimental than these novels; in addition, its analysis of English society is less mordant. And of course it does not possess the ethical complexity and technical and stylistic sophistication of the so-called major phase novels—*The Ambassadors, The Wings of the Dove,* and *The Golden Bowl.* Despite these differences, however, and its critical reputation, *The Tragic Muse* is a superb piece of realistic long prose fiction: tightly organized, despite its immense length; insightful in its treatment of both major and minor characters; continually illuminating in its dramatization of art "as a human complication and social stumbling block" (1:v); and continually interesting in its examination of "some of the personal consequences of the art-appetite raised and intensified, swollen to voracity" (1:xvi).

The critical consensus about James's handling of the Tragic Muse herself—Miriam Rooth—is generally positive. Nonetheless, a few readers (most significantly James in his preface) have found the growth of her acting reputation to be implausibly rapid. In opposition to this complaint, one might observe that she is not a star at the end and that great success remains only a possibility, although certainly a real one. She appears to have flown higher than she actually has largely because of James's method of viewing her rise. She is seen, for example, through the infatuated eyes of the diplomat Peter Sherringham (in scenes and dramatizations of his consciousness) and the flamboyant predictions of Gabriel Nash; her passion, dedication, and shrewdness are conveyed by her own words; and once James allows the reader brief access to her consciousness—her visit to the Théâtre Français at end of book 4. As the result of this method, the reader observes and should be impressed by her inherited beauty, intelligence, curiosity, pride, and capacity for hard work.

One also discerns how her environment—in particular her peripatetic and humiliating life with her mother—have provoked enough resentment to fuel a passion to succeed as well as a relatively ruthless willingness to use whatever or whomever she needs for success. During this period she has learned an attractive manner to mask her ruthlessness and has developed a skin thick enough to rebuff insults. In addition, her experience before the action begins has offered her many chances to observe: "Oh I've observed scenes between men and

women—very quiet, terribly quiet, but awful, pathetic, tragic! Once
I saw a woman do something that I'm going to do some day when I'm
great—if I can get the situation. I'll tell you what it is sometime—I'll
do it for you. Oh it *is* the book of life!" (1:200–201)

In addition to suggesting James's conception of the artist as a person
upon whom nothing is lost, passages like this suggest the influence of
Robert Browning's "Fra Lippo Lippi," a character who combines a similar attractive vulnerability with a single-minded drive not merely to
survive but to win. In James's portrait here the naturalistic influence
that pervades the novel is much in evidence. Like both Peter and the
politician-painter Nick Dormer, Miriam is not enacting decisions consciously made: her inherited characteristics and social background drive
her toward the top, an apex the reader is almost convinced she will
reach, even though by the end she has not come close to it. Parenthetically, the momentum and sense of inevitability experienced by the
reader because of James's method of presenting Miriam and the pattern
of success he establishes for her are also indications of the naturalistic
mode to which the novel in part belongs. Despite James's own reservations about his treatment of this character, therefore, her rise is an
example of skillful and successful foreshortening.

The Functions of Gabriel Nash

A great deal of the meager amount of critical controversy generated
by *The Tragic Muse* has centered on the enigmatic minor character
Gabriel Nash—someone whom James, surprisingly, does not even
mention in his preface. The majority of the discussion of Nash has
speculated about possible sources of his character—Henry James, Sr.,
for example, Oscar Wilde, James himself, Herbert Pratt (a friend of
William James), and so on—or has tried to reconcile the realistic treatment of Nash during most of the novel with the Hawthornesque fading
away of the portrait of him that Nick is painting and his own disappearance at the end of *The Tragic Muse*. One might remark about the
"source" of his character that—like almost all of James's creations—he
is undoubtedly a composite. With respect to the ending, one should
observe that the painting does not actually fade away: Nick Dormer
only imagines that it almost does, a "disappearance" convenient to him
at a point when he has received from Nash all the benefits he is likely
to garner from their friendship, and when Nick prepares to take up

again with his conservative fiancée, Julia Dallow, who despises Nash and the threat the aesthete-philosopher represents, from her point of view, to Nick's respectability and masculinity.

In his preface, James expresses his pride in the unobtrusive skill by which he has used Miriam Rooth to fuse the separate strands of the plot so as to prevent the novel from becoming a "baggy monster." At least as important in forging the unity is Gabriel Nash, because his direct or indirect influence is crucial in practically everything of importance that occurs in *The Tragic Muse*. He introduces Miriam to the old French actress who eventually tutors her, Madame Carré, as well as to Peter and Nick. He encourages Nick's dissatisfaction with politics and helps him to recognize his true vocation (Nash has this influence both early in the novel and, more crucially, after Nick has been elected as member to Crockhurst and has temporarily retreated to his London studio around Easter while Julia visits Harsh). Nash is a major cause of Nick's rupture with Julia because he brings Miriam as a model (after Nick had forgotten about the actress for several months), and because he stumbles into the studio as Julia is about to leave; one might even suggest that Julia is more disturbed by her fiancé's friendship with Gabriel than by his interest in Miriam. Nash helps to create the unbearable tension in Peter Sherringham—which eventually provokes his impetuous decision to seek a new diplomatic post—through his comments about Miriam's supposed love of Nick, about her need for a subservient husband, and through his predictions about her grotesque future. In sum, Nash has a very large influence upon the plots of *The Tragic Muse,* a fact not mentioned by critics, and one testifying to James's unostentatious structural skill.

Those readers who see in Gabriel Nash strong links with his creator frequently discuss Nash's importance as a spokesman for James's criticisms of English theatrical conditions, his ideas about the relationship between "being" and "doing," or his conviction that the individual should be true to his intrinsic talents. Certainly as a kind of Jamesian representative, Nash performs a significant function. Perhaps more important, because James handles Nash adroitly, the fiction is not "violated" by the ideas. Nash's criticisms about the lamentable English theatrical conditions, for example, or his predictions about the future of the drama are made in prickly scenes with Peter Sherringham, tense because of the fervor with which the diplomat often opposes Nash and the tight control through which Peter suppresses his distaste for him.

Despite his occasional repugnance for Nash as a person and for what his ideas and demeanor may represent, Peter does not want to be linked with his philistine sister, Julia Dallow.

Nash's comments about the importance of personal style, about the link between being and doing, about the need to discern, cultivate, and cherish one's talents, are made primarily in scenes with Nick, convincingly dramatic in their quiet exploration of the renewed friendship between these very different young men and in their revelation of a buried self in Nick that he has been trying to suppress. There is drama also in the occasional suggestions of a deep frustration in Nash himself, caused by the public reception of his ideas—a genuine pain usually masked by his effete persona: "Yes, I've encountered men and women who thought you impudent if you weren't simply so stupid as they. The only impudence is unprovoked, or even mere dull, aggression, and I indignantly protest that I'm never guilty of *that* clumsiness. Ah for what do they take one, with *their* beastly⁵ presumption?" (1:171).

Noteworthy also about James's use of Nash as a quasi-spokesman is the author's continual undercutting of reader expectations about how Nash should be presented. At the beginning of the novel, James refuses to pander to the *Punch* stereotype of the affected aesthete: many of Nash's ideas are cogent and, as a result, characters who observe nothing in him, like Lady Agnes or Julia Dallow, seem narrow. Yet, a hint of the ridiculous always hovers about Nash, and thus it is impossible to identify completely with him or to believe he speaks totally for the author. When Nash asserts the wisdom of acting in harmony with the promptings of one's intuitively sensed needs rather than in response to more conventionally admirable and rationally defensible reasons, he seems insightful. Yet a purpose of the novel is to challenge these insights—to show the reader, for example, how difficult it may be to understand one's needs, to dramatize how particular needs may conflict (in oneself as well as with others), and to point out how ephemeral this communication with a buried resource may be. Moreover, the reader also discerns a hint of the specious in Nash's defense of being as opposed to doing: the young man has a taste for showy gestures supposedly provoked by the pulses of pure being and a distaste for the grubbiness often involved in doing well—a dislike confirmed by his loss of interest in Nick's work near the end of the novel.⁶

By the end also the reader may suspect that the reasons for Nash's unconventional ideas are essentially negative—a fear of being fixed (in an attitude, a friendship, a personality), or a compulsion to react against something (ideas of conventional people, for example) rather than on behalf of something else. In Nash, James has taken a flat character and given him roundness. Through his handling of Nash, James has also kept his reader off balance, thereby involving him in judging the value and validity of ideas about which he as creator cares passionately. One of the best examples of James's skill in *The Tragic Muse,* therefore, is his treatment of Gabriel Nash.

The Second Half of the Novel

Evidence of this skill also exists in his treatment of both Nick Dormer and Peter Sherringham in the much maligned second half of the novel. Sherringham is arguably one of the most interesting characters ever created by James. In essence, he is an ironic portrait of someone who appears to be or should be (given his diplomatic profession) under control, but who is not, and a character whose actions are frequently driven by motives he neither understands nor acknowledges. There are several ways of expressing the general conflict that sunders Peter's personality: one might refer, for example, to his French and English sides, or his unconventional and conventional. Subsumed under each of these general divisions are particular ones: his "liberal" attitude toward women, for example, as opposed to his wish for females to support his manly point of view; his tolerance of those belonging to inferior social classes and his feeling that they are inferior (Peter is in essence a snob although part of him abhors snobbishness). The conflict is displayed in the relation between his avocation—the theater—and his profession—diplomacy; and his desire to mediate between these poles is shown in the careful, self-conscious way in which he indulges his interest in the theater. He loves the aesthetic appeal of the Comédie Française and the tradition that permeates it; yet he dislikes discussion of theatrical techniques—of the elements that make it a craft rather than an art. He finds particularly repugnant the cool dissection performed upon French actresses by male theatrical critics. He also abhors the supposed vulgarity of certain aspects of the profession: the audience's need to lionize, the irregular social life, the proclivity of the stars whom he admires to associate with the lesser figures whom he mistrusts.

The essential conflict along with its individual ramifications achieves intense focus in Peter's infatuation with Miriam. As he comes to realize, he has been attracted to her since their first meeting, probably because of her unusual beauty and his immediate intuition of her dramatic gift. At the same time he is repelled by her crude, pushy vulgarity and the extremely rough covering that hides her talent. Although part of him is repelled, Peter encourages Madame Carré to give Miriam lessons and begins to play Pygmalion himself, not only because of her beauty and incipient skill, but also for other reasons that become important: his intuition of a forceful and admirable person beneath her crudeness, her vulnerability and willingness to exploit it (Miriam recognizes the appeal of the vulnerable to Peter and plays up to it throughout the novel), the fact that Gabriel Nash condescends to her (Peter's unacknowledged hostility toward Nash has an important effect on several decisions). The reader observes how several of these motives are unconscious.

One should observe also how almost all of Peter's actions related to Miriam are influenced by needs, drives, conflicts he does not seem really to understand. His request for a change of diplomatic venue, for example, is made impetuously—primarily out of fear, distaste, extreme frustration rather than calculation. What seems to happen is that Miriam's appeal to the unconventional part of Peter's self becomes so powerful that the conventional—and ultimately dominant part—asserts itself and causes action, or more accurately, reaction. From this point until the end when, because of Miriam's marriage, he is almost compelled to marry Nick's sister Biddy (an only superficially liberated young woman whose "unconventional" ideas are formed largely because of a conventional worship of her older brother), Peter continually vacillates between his two "selves" as they respond to or react against what Miriam represents. In the two remarkable and passionate confrontation scenes with the actress in the novel's second half, for example, one cannot help but observe how many of Peter's responses are improvised—forced out of him by ambivalent responses to Miriam's personality.

In chapter 41 Peter visits Miriam, at her request, the evening prior to her performance. Initially he intends to talk over her role with her and then depart. As they converse, however—and as she expresses in tantalizing fashion her appreciation of his help, sincere concern about his career, regrets about her selfishness and predictions about a future miserable marriage for herself—he is driven to express his love and almost to propose to her (2:254). Subsequently, Peter reveals an awkward and desperate passion: "You have, as it happens, a personal charm for me that no one has ever approached, and from the top of your splendid head to the sole of your theatrical shoe (I could go down on my face—there, abjectly—and kiss it!) every inch of you is dear and delightful to me" (2:257-58).

Throughout this scene the reader is puzzled by Miriam's own motives: is she playing a role? does she begin by playing a role and then grow into it until it becomes real? does she want Peter to propose to her? It is impossible to decide both here and later, and the resulting mystery of her performance adds another shade to James's portrait of the actress as lady, lady as actress.

Growing in Peter, in response to this scene and earlier signs of Miriam's versatility, is an awareness of her potential to become a lady in his sense of this word; growing in him, therefore, is a vision of compromise that will reconcile the needs of his competing selves: he will ask her unequivocally to become the wife of a diplomat. Flushed with this vision and made ecstatic by her triumph on opening night, Peter performs the totally undiplomatic act of demanding that she keep her admirers waiting while she visits him, without a chaperon, at St. John's Wood. Here again, in this lengthy occasion in chapter 46, the reader observes how much of what Peter says appears to be improvised, as Miriam batters against his arguments with her beauty, passion, and intelligence. Peter is so entranced by Miriam that her proposal that he renounce his career in order to marry her briefly becomes a real possibility, as does her bizarre suggestion that Peter become an actor, or finally, that he learn how to act while on his new diplomatic posting and then return to her. Peter resists Miriam's attempts to create her own ideal compromise, but he does so not so much through conscious, rational choice as stubborn, irrational hostility against the theater and the threat posed by it to his deepest, "English" self.

This is a long, magnificently structured occasion, one in which James dramatizes ideas crucial to himself—about the theater, about identity, about the ways in which human relationships can aid and hinder the discovery of individuality and proper vocations—through the subtly choreographed argument of two fully realized characters.

What needs to be stressed about this sequence is that the debate is not weighted strongly on either side: Peter's argument that Miriam's dramatic self could be realized best in a diplomat's setting seems for the moment plausible—particularly in light of the vapid English theater; and Miriam's contemptuous dismissal of the diplomatic milieu— "I've seen them abroad—the dreariest females—and could imitate them here" (2:374)—is made to seem only partially valid. Her own proposal that Peter should renounce his vocation so as to help her and the English stage also makes momentary sense. In sum, the dialectic seems genuine, like Bernard Shaw at his best: neither character is merely a spokesman for James. Worth observing also is the manner in which, finally, the confrontation provokes both characters into finding and expressing their deepest selves: Peter loves Miriam but his strong distaste for aspects of the theater combined with his attitude toward the proper roles of men and women must prevent him from marrying her. Miriam at the end no longer seems to be acting: she is attracted to Peter, but her compulsion to succeed on her own terms combined with her aspirations for the theater in general cause her to reject his offer.

A final point about this chapter is that James has improved an extremely impressive 1890 version of it through the revisions he made for the New York Edition. Several changes are of the "stage direction" type: descriptions are added so that the reader can better visualize the scene, imagine the rhythm of the interchanges, or hear the voices of the lover/combatants. Other changes make Peter seem stronger and less pitiable, more determined, and more genuinely sympathetic than the 1890 text. Thus, in the New York Edition, Sherringham replied "with a ring that spoke enough of his sincerity" (2:339) rather than "poor Peter pursued, with a soft quaver that betrayed all his sincerity" (507).[7] Or, in the later text, "Peter proceeded with a still, deep heat that kept down in a manner his rising scorn and exasperated passion" (2:341) rather than "Sherringham went on, with rising scorn and exasperated passion" (508).

Analogously, Miriam's relationship with him is made to appear less purely adversarial, more genuinely disturbed and even loving. Thus, her reply to a particularly vexatious argument in the later text is "'vain words, vain words, my dear!' and she turned off again in her impatience" (2:344) as opposed to "'Rubbish, rubbish!' Miriam mocked" (510). Or a comment by Miriam "deepened his wound" (2:346) rather than "twisted the weapon in" (512). In part because of revisions such as this, the scene should be responded to as a moving, almost tragic confrontation between fully realized characters and understandable but inimical views of life. Peter never really comprehends either why he is attracted so deeply to Miriam or why, finally, he is repelled by her, but the reader should. And the reader should also discern how difficult it will be for Peter ever to control her appeal for him. It is therefore fitting that his infatuation should be ended by Miriam's marriage to

Basil Dashwood: for someone who is, beneath his liberality, as deeply conventional as Peter, the effect of the marriage is like sand thrown upon flames.

A problem created in *The Tragic Muse* by James's focus on Peter and his tempestuous relationship with Miriam is that, after he flees London, the shift of attention to Nick, his low-keyed style, and his muted relationship with Miriam must be a letdown to the reader. Moreover, the novel's book 8 covers a longer period of historical time, contains fewer developed scenes, and depends more upon analysis of one character's consciousness than any sequence of comparable length in the novel. Thus, the ending may seem hurried to some readers—a quick tidying up and twisting together of threads already spun out to significant length. Having admitted this, one should also point out that there is a great deal in this section to maintain reader interest: the quiet and inevitable rupture between Nick and Miriam, the break between Nick and Nash, the gradual and painful reestablishing of relationships between Nick, his family, and Julia. The consequences of the "swollen art appetite" are here relatively undramatic; they are, nonetheless, as plausible a part of the story as the more theatrical gestures that have punctuated the two plots earlier in the novel. James apologizes in his preface when he admits his failure to make Nick "quite as interesting as he was fondly intended to be" (1:xxi). Given Nick's distrust of his "cleverness," however, his respect for talent carefully nurtured, and his need to create pictures of which he himself may be proud, it is almost mandatory that he be presented so unostentatiously.

James sets out to create a character deeply divided between the appeal of art and the conservative influence of a traditional world; in a sense, Nick is a Roderick Hudson who has been bred differently. The possibilities for grand dissipation or precipitate and idiosyncratic self-development are not in Nick; neither is there in his essential nature (his heredity) nor in his background (his environment) an ingredient that might have pushed him toward becoming a painter in one of the experimental modes. His radicalism, therefore, must express itself in a conservative manner. As a result, by the end of the novel we see how the influences of the "world"—Nick's family, the attraction of Julia, the comfort of the country house in which he was raised, his distaste for the romantic but cold garret, his inability to potboil to keep himself out of it—are combining with his talent and respect for artistic achievement of a classical kind to move him toward what will probably be a marriage with Julia and a respectable career as a portrait painter.

The kind of ideal compromise, therefore, that Peter Sherringham was unable to achieve seems possible for Nick. Yet James makes no predictions about Nick's future; because of the character James has created, he really does not know how Nick will turn out.

A final topic worthy of discussion before concluding this defense of *The Tragic Muse* is James's subtle, convincing treatment of Nick as would-be politician. In responding to this dimension of the novel, Donald Stone complains that, for James, seemingly only "personal good looks and a flair for rhetoric" are important to a political career. So too, the novel suggests, are family connections and traditions, youth and health, personal charm, the proper education, a love of competition, and money. All these factors are quickly added to James's plausible sketch of Nick's political potential. Also crucial as an impetus to political success is timing, an element not emphasized but nonetheless present in the novel. Although a reader cannot be certain precisely when—with respect to historical time—Nick runs in the by-election for the House of Commons seat after the death of Mr. Pinks (1:51), one can surmise from details provided by James that the election takes place some time in the summer of either 1887, 1888, or 1889 (probably 1887). The exact date does not matter. What is significant, however, is that during these years the Liberal party was in disarray over questions of leadership and policy, problems that James's letters of the time reflect both his knowledge of and interest in. In July 1886 the then prime minister, William Gladstone, was defeated, primarily because he supported Home Rule for Ireland, a policy he had sprung upon the Liberal party suddenly and that generated much hostility within the party and the country as a whole. During the period of the novel, the Liberals moved out of power (they were not elected again until 1891), and many Liberal supporters—particularly members of the upper class—were anxious to find a new leader, not only because of Gladstone's Home Rule policy, but also because he was a very old man.

In alluding to Nick Dormer's contest for the riding of Crockhurst, the narrator refers to the Liberal party's great interest in the outcome of the election. The interest is understandable. Given the almost desperate need of the Liberal party for new leadership, given Nick's pedigree and financial support, and given the actual Conservative example in Parliament of the youthful Randolph Churchill (for whom a magnificent future was being predicted), the potential of someone like Nick would have been unlimited. James does not complicate his novel needlessly by telling his reader which point of view—about Ireland, for example—Nick might have supported. Instead, the novelist suggests his character's capacity for idealism, then alludes to his growing skepticism and disillusionment with party politics—feelings characteristic of many Liberals during these years. To paraphrase T. S. Eliot again: James's fine mind does not allow particular political ideas to violate his conception of Nick—the young man of high promise groping for a satisfying vocation while trying to unite his competing selves. Yet, the political background is present and important—not of crucial importance, of course—just another shade in the subtly modulated picture of several young people attempting to reconcile art with the world.

Chapter Four
The Theatrical Years and After

Almost a decade elapsed between the publication of *The Tragic Muse* and James's next novel, *The Awkward Age*. Even before beginning work on *Muse* James had hoped that, after finishing it, he could support himself writing short fiction. Then, while in Paris in December 1888, a proposal from the actor-producer Edward Compton that James prepare a stage version of *The American* aroused his enthusiasm for the theater again. (In 1881 and 1882 he had failed in his attempts to have produced a play version of *Daisy Miller*.) While completing *The Tragic Muse* James wrote two acts of *The American* and mailed them to Compton for his perusal. Refurbished with a happy ending, the play opened near Liverpool in January 1891 and eventually achieved a modest success in London in the fall of 1891 with Elizabeth Robins, notorious because of her performances as Ibsen's "bad heroines," somewhat miscast as Claire de Cintré. By the spring of 1890 James had decided to confine himself to short fiction and drama, which he did for more than four years.

Despite the deaths during these years of several people with whom he had been more or less intimate, most notably his sister Alice and his writer friend Constance Fenimore Woolson (a probable suicide), James's life seems to have been relatively happy, in large part because he found the alternation between short fiction and the theater immensely satisfying. James was extremely successful in placing his stories—eighteen tales, including "The Pupil," "The Real Thing," and "The Middle Years," more than in any comparable period in his career. Moreover, particularly after he had arranged for the production of the historical costume drama *Guy Domville,* he was almost convinced of his ability to write serious and popular plays—to reconcile Drama with the Theatre; this was a dream cherished not only by several characters in *The Tragic Muse* but also by many would-be reformers of the English stage, such as George Bernard Shaw. Enthused by the example of Henrik Ibsen, whose plays the novelist learned to admire after an initial repugnance, and believing himself to be mastering the techniques of this new fascinating medium, James showed constant evidence of his faith in eventual success.[1]

Guy Domville failed, unfortunately, after a fairly short run that began in early January 1895. Despite this failure, however, and his humiliation on opening night (when, at the end of the performance, his appearance on stage was greeted by a cacophony of cheers and hisses), James soon after began work on a play for Ellen Terry, the female lead in *Guy Domville,* who had asked him for something for her American tour.[2]

The danger for the critic in examining this period in James's career is to exaggerate its pathos and tragedy. If we are tempted to do this, we should observe that James quickly picked himself off the floor, aided significantly by his ability to rationalize (he told his brother William that only the rabble had hated *Guy Domville*; it was clearly his best work and he would arrange for it to be published, which he did) Significant also were several other factors: the support from many friends and admirers, the money he made from his play, the legacy of $20,000 from Alice's estate that he had to fall back on, and the continued success of his short fiction.

Soon after his theatrical failure he published "The Next Time" in the *Yellow Book,* an aesthetic journal published by an admirer, Henry Harland, in which two earlier stories had appeared. This one was a rueful and ironic tale about a serious writer unable to pander to popular tastes, despite his eagerness to do so. About the same time James was asked for three stories by Horace Scudder, the editor of the *Atlantic Monthly.* As a step toward meeting this obligation, James's conscious plan was to base one of the tales on an anecdote he had heard about a family lawsuit centering around the legacy of precious furniture. James's unconscious need, however, seems to have been to write something much more substantial than the very short stories that had been his typical fare for several years and that he was supposed to write for Scudder. Thus James wrestled unsuccessfully for several months in complex *Notebooks* entries to curb the story's length, and thus the short tale (originally called "The House Beautiful") became first the 75,000-word, seven-installment story "The Old Things" and eventually the novella *The Spoils of Poynton.*

Although this novella was not the "large and confident action," the "splendid and supreme creation" James said in his 14 February 1895 notebook entry he would some day like to write, the *Spoils* was "large" enough to permit the use of two important methods: "pure, dense, summarized narration" (as he wrote in his notebook), the dominant method used for several years to compose very short fiction; and lengthy scenes told primarily through dialogue. Although this latter technique was a novelistic staple in James's pretheatrical period, he had not written such fully developed scenes in fiction for approximately five years.

The precise influence of James's theatrical experience on his later long fiction is difficult to determine.[3] Certainly this experience encouraged him to write "scenarios"—careful preliminary plans that were much longer and more detailed than earlier had been his practice. James's pious hope was that the scenarios would help cure his fictional elephantiasis. That they usually failed to do this, however, is suggested by the several ostensibly small ideas that grew into large books. It is also doubtful whether writing two mediocre producible plays and several unproducible ones taught him the value of carefully organized and well-developed scenes in fiction. On the contrary, almost from the beginning of his career he recognized this value; all of his novels contain long, well-structured sequences, confined in space and time, whose action is advanced primarily through dialogue. Nor, arguably, did he learn from the theater how to discover and isolate those moments in scenes that help create and explain changes in mood and tempo. Although James's talk of "hinges" of scenes in his *Notebooks* and his likening of sections of his fiction to scenes and acts of a play, as he does in his *Notebooks* and the preface to *The Awkward Age,* show that he had learned theatrical terminology, an analysis of earlier novels reveals that he had always known about "hinges"; he simply did not know what to call them.

James's posttheater novels contain significantly less interpretive and discursive narrative commentary than his earlier ones and proportionally more of the "stage direction" variety. Yet the most important element for creating the best scenes in his later long fiction is present in the earlier: James's willingness, even eagerness, to use the fully prepared for and developed scene—the "occasion," as he calls it in the preface to *The Awkward Age*—as a technique of discovery. When James "gets, for further intensity into the very skin" of his characters (to quote his 1902 essay on Balzac),[4] and by so doing allows them to respond thoroughly to charged circumstances, he also invites them to become more round as they bring to the surface what is latent.

Certainly there are technical differences between James's posttheater and pretheater fiction, but the differences are, arguably, matters of degree and combination, rather than kind. Between the failure of *Guy Domville* in early 1895 and the book publication of *The Awkward Age* in spring 1899, James published five novellas: *The Spoils of Poynton, The Other House, What Maisie Knew, The Turn of the Screw,* and *In the Cage.* The influence of the theater is particularly obvious in *The Other House,* originally conceived as a play, because it contains much more dialogue and much less summarized narration than any James novel or novella except *The Awkward Age.* On the other hand, this work is not a particularly impressive achievement.

In *The Spoils of Poynton, What Maisie Knew,* and *In the Cage*—a story about a telegraphist's vicarious involvement with an upper-class affair, written just before *The Awkward Age*—the third-person point of view is more rigorously limited to the perspective of a single character than in the earlier long fiction. On the other hand, James in the earlier fiction had sometimes depended upon a dominant point-of-view character (Hyacinth Robinson, for example, or Rowland Mallet in *Roderick Hudson*), though not so consistently. Before writing *The Turn of the Screw* James had published more than forty stories told from the perspective of a first-person narrator; almost all, however, except for "The Aspern Papers," are much shorter than the story about the governess and the supposedly haunted children.

It is true that James's style differentiates all of the posttheater novellas from the pretheater fiction: to oversimplify considerably, one can observe in the later fiction a greater proportion of abstract nouns, for example, of daring and unusual imagery, of complicated and unconventional sentence structures.[5] Although probably accelerated during the composition of *Maisie* when, in February 1897, James began to dictate his fiction to a typist because of pain in his right wrist, these changes evolve gradually and can be observed in the short fiction written during the theatrical years. In sum, the effect of James's experience in the theater on the formal qualities of his fiction is probably less great—less "experimental"—than it has been the critical fashion in recent years to maintain. On the other hand, one profound effect of his theatrical failure is so utterly mundane and obvious that—like the location of the purloined letter in Poe's story—it has been ignored: James was encouraged, for reasons of finance, and compelled, for reasons of pride and self-esteem, to write stories again whose length could not be encompassed in one or two issues of a magazine. His enforced reinvolvement in longer fiction led eventually to the composition of *The Awkward Age, The Ambassadors, The Wings of the Dove,* and *The Golden Bowl.*

Chapter Five

The Awkward Age:
Artificial Form and Human
Reality

Background

Genesis and text.   The most important nonliterary events between the publication of *What Maisie Knew* in September 1897 and James's initial work on *The Awkward Age* in late summer 1898 were his successful negotiation of a twenty-one-year lease on Lamb House, Rye, just after *Maisie* was published, and his move to this arcadia in Sussex in early June of the next year. In the interim James maintained a typically frantic literary schedule in that he published several short stories and novellas (most notably *The Turn of the Screw*), and negotiated contracts for further projects (*In the Cage,* for example); for a time he also wrote a column of literary commentary and book reviews (e.g., on Walt Whitman's "Calamus" and "The Wound Dresser") entitled "American Letters" for a new journal called *Literature,* a precursor of *TLS.* Given this schedule it is not surprising that "The Great Good Place," a story written just prior to his move to Lamb House, embodies a thinly disguised longing for a haven of rest.

Despite a gorgeous summer and many convivial guests at his new home, James there completed *In the Cage* and later, under great pressure, *The Awkward Age.*[1] According to letters, James did not finish the serial version of the novel until some time in December, for a serialization in *Harper's Weekly* that concluded on 7 January. Then, prior to leaving for a vacation on the Continent, he remained at Lamb House in January and February, reading proofs and revising the novel for its English and American editions.

The Awkward Age appeared almost continuously in serial form from 1 October 1898 to 7 January 1899. No episode appeared in the 17 December "Christmas number," so that, according to an editor's note, the issue could be complete in itself; it is quite possible, however, that James did not have his weekly installment ready in time. The first British edition, of 2,000 copies, was published on 25 April 1899 by William Heinemann, James's friend from the theatrical years and an Ibsenite, who had begun to publish James's work in 1895 with *Terminations,* a collection of short stories. The first American edition of 1,000 copies was published by Harper's on 12 May.[2] The final version of the text is volume 9 of the New York Edition, published by Scribner's in 1908.

Although the scholarly assumption has been that James revised his novel only once between the serial and the first British and American editions, in actual fact the American text seems to be an earlier, less careful revision of the serial than the British, even though the American edition was published later. There is really only one significant difference between the serial and the first American edition: the latter is divided into ten books named after various characters; in the former, there is only an occasional correspondence between the serial episodes and the "books" focusing on particular characters. There are also a few other minor revisions—the elimination of commas, for example, a few changes in spelling, an occasional change in wording.

Noteworthy among the many verbal changes for the British edition are two made at the end of the first chapter of the "Tishy Grendon" book (book 8). Here, Vanderbank probes the heroine Nanda hard about her knowledge of the risqué French novel that he has discovered with his name written on it, but not in his hand. In both the serial and first American editions, Vanderbank queries, "And may I ask if you've read the work?" and then, "And read the thing?"[3] In the British edition, he says, "And may I ask if you've read the remarkable work." Then the irony of this response (by which he tries to maintain his insouciance) collapses into the real perturbation of the following: "And read the confounded thing?" (301). This dialogue is unchanged for the New York Edition (397).

For the New York Edition, James, using the British text as he revised, made a few more changes in punctuation, changed the numbering of the chapters by making it continuous within each book (thus reinforcing the sense of the unity of each "occasion"), and made a number of verbal emendations. In the first chapter, for example, the narrative comment, "Vanderbank felt positively more guilty than he would have expected" (8), becomes "ever so much more guilty" (12). The change underlines the younger man's feelings of guilt in the presence of Longdon, the older visitor from the country: Vanderbank is bothered by his own behavior and that of his London friends and is challenged by the older man's presence.

Source and influence. The donnée upon which the novel is based first appeared in James's *Notebooks* only several months after his theatrical failure. Alluded to in the entry are the problems posed for a "free-talking young mother" by the presence of her seventeen- or eighteen-year-old daughter; also mentioned are a young man who is a friend of the mother and attracted to the girl although appalled by her circumstances, and a contrasting "foreignized friend or sister, who has married her daughter, very virtuously and very badly, unhappily, just to get her out of the atmosphere of her own talk and entourage—and takes my little lady to task for her inferior system and inferior virtue" (192). This idea may have come from James's reading of magazine articles devoted to problems of English manners, or, as he suggests in the preface, from his own observations.

In any event, there are probably many influences either leading to or reflected in *The Awkward Age*. Several critics have argued that the contrast between Mr. Longdon's Beccles and Mrs. Brookingham's (or Mrs. "Brook's") Buckingham Crescent, a contrast not mentioned in the *Notebooks* entry written before James had seen Lamb House at Rye, reflects the author's sense of the difference between the relatively placid historicity of Suffolk and the frantic modernity of London. Reflected also in James's portrayal of Longdon is undoubtedly his own occasional fifty-five-year-old sense of being part of a moribund generation—one whose values contrasted with and had been perhaps superseded by those advertised in the newspapers and divorce courts—and dramatized in the recent *What Maisie Knew*.

Certain literary sources may also have influenced this essential contrast, such as that between Célimène and Alçeste in Molière's *Misanthrope*; more generally, the contrasts between sophisticated and naive manners, urban and rural, relative youth and age, that one identifies with the comedy of manners, were probably suggested to James by the quasi-dramatic medium in which he was working. One might also see mirrored in this contrast an "international" one between an innocent American and experienced Europeans; James calls attention to this parallel by having Longdon refer to himself as Rip Van Winkle.

A similar potpourri of possible sources may be discerned if one looks closely at other aspects of the novel: most plausibly Balzac, for example (for the way in which the extreme emotions of melodrama penetrate the controlled surface of manners); Thackeray (in the ambivalent Becky Sharpe–like portrait of Mrs. Brook); even Shakespeare or the flawed but charismatic heroines of certain Jacobean dramatists. There are also many echoes of James's own work in *The Awkward Age* and parallels in characters and relationships between this novel and his earlier fiction. The ostensibly chaste but potentially sexual relation between Longdon and Nanda, for example—what Strother Purdy has likened to Nabo-kov's Humbert Humbert and Lolita—is anticipated in the very early *Watch and Ward*. Nanda is reminiscent of many Jamesian nice young girls or of an almost grownup Maisie Farange. The vacillating young man—Vanderbank here—appears repeatedly in James's fiction from the beginning of his career, most recently in Sir Claude of *What Maisie Knew* and Tony Breame of *The Other House*.

James's 1890 fiction anticipates *The Awkward Age* in other ways as well. One notes, for example, his fascination with the question of pa-rental or quasi-parental influence on the young, an early interest that becomes central in "The Pupil," *What Maisie Knew,* and *The Turn of the Screw.*[4] And there are other common concerns: with the way in which problems of epistemology can complicate behavior, as in the fiction just mentioned and *In the Cage*; with the relation between sexuality and ethics, an interest that becomes almost obsessive during these years; with the masculinization of women and decline of the aristocracy.[5]

As for the form of the novel, James in his preface mentions his desire to emulate the French writer "Gyp," whose novels in dialogue were popular (as was the dialogue fiction of several other authors).[6] Ob-viously relevant also are James's plays-turned-into-fiction, *The Other House* and, most recently, "Covering End." His experience with these stories helped him to write *The Awkward Age* quickly and skillfully. More generally, as has been suggested earlier, his experiments with the 1890s novellas in making interpretive demands of a different kind and greater difficulty from those made by his contemporaries are obvious "sources" for this long work's frequently elliptical dialogue, reticent narration, and equivocal handling of plot details and character motivation.

Ambiguity, Dramatic Form, and the Priestess of the Temple

In a letter written to his friend Paul Bourget while working on *The Awkward Age,* James chides the successful French novelist for being too obvious, a quality that is "an injury to the patches of ambiguity and the abysses of shadow which really are the clothing—or much of it of the *effects* that constitute the material of our trade."[7] A major cause of the ambiguity in James's own novel is its peculiar form: less frequently than in his other works does he either "go behind" his characters or comment directly as narrator about their behavior; instead, as methods of characterization and aids to interpretation he depends primarily upon dialogue and a kind of ideal observer of the scenes who provides the reader with vital information about setting, characters' appearances, movements, and tones of voice.[8] In a sense, James's technique enables us to experience a difficulty encountered by most of his characters—that of linking signs, linguistic and behavioral, to character. Almost bereft of the conventional support of narrator commentary, doubtful at times even about the trustworthiness of an ostensible raissoneur figure—the perplexed middle-aged visitor from Suffolk, Mr. Longdon—the reader is forced by James to peer and ponder, not so much like a spectator at a play, as like a person in real life who must organize his behavior in response to evidence that cannot quite be trusted.

The quasi-dramatic form of *The Awkward Age* is particularly appropriate for suggesting the character of the London coterie's leader, Mrs. Brook: to her, reality is theatrical. At times, for example, she sees herself as a great lady in a classic French comedy of manners (because one must avoid "cheap paradox," it is probably not a comedy by Oscar Wilde); to Mrs. Brook, Buckingham Crescent is a "temple of talk" to whom favorites come for solace and stimulation. That this image is to a certain extent distorted is revealed by the relative lack of cleverness in the conversation between her and the most important members of her set, Mitchy, the wealthy businessman, and Vanderbank. On the other hand, some of the talk is witty, although her best lines are uttered in catty conversation with the Duchess, who is not part of her group.

A problem presented for the reader in understanding and evaluating the behavior of Mrs. Brook is that she quite consciously tries to prevent other people—perhaps even herself—from discovering the relation between her words and her character.[9] Nonetheless, a few plausible guesses can be hazarded about her. It is clear, for example, that she is jealous of her daughter and desirous of catering to her own needs; it is not equally clear, but nonetheless suggested that, in a confused, inadequately understood, but partially genuine fashion, she wants to be a good mother. Thus, she is being only partially hyperbolic when she says to Van about Nanda's prospects for marriage, "Only it's just from the depth of my thought for my daughter's happiness that I've clung to this resource. He [Mitchy] would so absolutely, so unreservedly do anything for her." The possibility that Nanda's unconventional looks and peculiar style may make her unmarriageable is a worry to Mrs. Brook—as well as being a real problem in a family with affluent tastes and meager funds, an older son with talent only for sponging, and two younger children who some day will create problems of their own.

Mitchy, who for a period seems a possible husband for Nanda, is eventually disqualified because of the young girl's attitude toward him. From Mrs. Brook's point of view, a marriage to Vanderbank is out of the question, not only because of her attraction to him but also because, as she says to Van's face, he could not bring himself to marry Nanda (book 6, chapter 2). It is never fully explained why Mrs. Brook makes this prediction, although she says that he will never allow himself to be seen as taking a bribe from Mr. Longdon for marrying Nanda. Her conclusion, however, may be based on a shrewd reading of Van's character: because of his peculiar scruples—of which she has firsthand experience in her tantalizing but ultimately frustrating and probably nonconsummated relationship with him—he will not marry any woman who may be soiled (see 378). Given the unlikelihood of Van as a husband, Mrs. Brook's strategy in trying to "work" Mr. Longdon (and make him a benefactor for her daughter) is perfectly understandable. One might even argue that the strategy is admirable because of Nanda's affection for Longdon, his kindness, and the fact that he will not live forever.

It would be fatuous to sentimentalize Mrs. Brook's character. Certainly James does not, as is demonstrated by the ubiquitous and malign presence of her son Harold, in that Harold is in part her responsibility. But, in addition to her wit, "pluck" (91), and wonderful ability to face down embarrassing predicaments, Mrs. Brook is not totally selfish. Certainly at times she seems frivolous, predatory, perhaps physically unfaithful to her husband. Yet James constantly undercuts our impulse to righteousness in responding to Mrs. Brook by making us see that this is the way of the world. Mrs. Brook is no reformer and she, like all of James's quasi-artists, tries to create something consonant with her sense of decorum—moral and aesthetic—out of the relatively meager elements at her disposal, elements that include several men seemingly incapable of love or healthy passion.

One other dimension worth remarking in James's treatment of Mrs. Brook is her relationships with her cousin-in-law, the Duchess, and with Mr. Longdon. Mrs. Brook is very bothered by the Duchess: not only does she have money and freedom, but the niece of the Duchess, little Aggie, is more marriageable than Nanda. It is also clear that Mr. Longdon's disapproval irritates Mrs. Brook because, despite her aplomb, she is at times disturbed by the contrast between herself and the images created by Longdon of her mother (Lady Julia) and daughter (see, for example, 318, 407, 409). Nanda, of course, is not the only person in the novel who is at an "awkward age." For these reasons, one of Mrs. Brook's motives, perhaps unconscious, in the frequently analyzed scene at Tishy Grendon's in book 8, when Mrs. Brook tells Longdon that Nanda must return from visiting Beccles, is that she wants to show him, the Duchess, and perhaps herself that she is a good mother and that this fact cannot be ignored. Parenthetically, her demand here seems improvised (not, as some critics have argued, planned beforehand), and improvised in response to happenings in the scene. Those that bother her most are her renewed sense (she has not seen Longdon for several months) that the older man disapproves of her, her envy of the Duchess's success in marrying Aggie (despite evidence that the marriage is not working), her jealousy of Nanda,[10] and her belief that the destruction of her own circle is imminent. Mrs. Brook compensates for her feelings of frustration and impotence by asserting her power and revealing her need both to be and appear to be a good mother: Nanda will return home.

An Odd Couple

Several critics have discerned in Nanda a person much more unsavory than on the surface she appears to be—in particular in the supposed masochism of her relation with Mitchy and in the supposed smugness and presumptuousness that she displays in trying to arrange her mother's future at the end of the novel. A more sensible and sensitive response might be to interpret Nanda's pleas that her mother's friends not abandon her as deriving from a genuine desire to compel commitment from weak men inclined to shirk responsibility. Moreover, although Nanda's standards may be somewhat naive or misguided (as in her desire to "save" Mitchy by encouraging his marriage to Aggie), her actions seem provoked by essentially admirable motives. Arguably her requests to Van and Mitchy reflect more on the men and the times than on her own inadequacies.[11] As for Mitchy's contention that Nanda cannot love anyone who does not disapprove of her (358), even if true, this attitude is surely more pathetic than reprehensible. Because she has been exposed to the promiscuous world of Tishy Grendon, Carrie Donner, and Fanny Cashmore, Nanda at times feels like "a sort of little drain-pipe with everything flowing through" (358); in essence, she no longer feels clean, and yearns for the cathartic quasi-paternal disapproval that she has not provoked from her own nonentity of a father. Moreover, her need to be disapproved of does not express itself in virulently pathological behavior: she would marry Vanderbank and he seems, despite his weakness, relatively well-adjusted.

Nanda goes with Longdon at the end of the novel because she likes him, she wants a rest, and she loves Beccles. Moreover, although some critics have read sterility into this choice, James's descriptions of Longdon's estate suggest a healthy, thriving tradition: things—such as the flowers that adorn Nanda's room at the end of the novel (496)—grow at Beccles. Another point is that Nanda may be attracted in an unacknowledged sexual way to Longdon. (An early reviewer thought the two would marry.) He is, after all, neither infirm nor aged. One might even argue that he is actually the most masculine male in the novel. Neither is she a "nymphet." Her refusal to marry Mitchy or permit herself to be touched by him near the conclusion of *The Awkward Age* is not motivated by cold prudery. She is not attracted to him sexually, perhaps because she intuits through her observation of him and Lord Petherton that he may be homosexual.[12] Certainly she discerns something wrong in this "friendship" (she says to Mitchy, "He preys upon you" [361]); she also hopes—naively but almost desperately, because she likes Mitchy a great deal—that Aggie can "save" (362) him from his most self-destructive inclinations.

Longdon also is not a prude, although he suspects that he is and partly blames himself for being prudish; nor is his final rejection of Buckingham Crescent narrowly moralistic. James, in fact, repeatedly makes the reader aware of the conflict between Longdon's impulse to condemn this new society and his equally strong impulse to be accepted by it, in part because he blames his failure to marry on an ingrained inability to seize the day (see 35, 218–19). Because he vacillates during much of the novel, his final and unequivocal rejection of this new world should seem more meaningful to the reader. Whether or not his incandescent image of Nanda's grandmother, Lady Julia, is accurate is insignificant. What is important is that it sustains him and causes no harm. By the time he brings Nanda to Beccles he seems no longer to be thinking of—or at least talking about—her resemblance to Lady Julia. Longdon feels affection for Nanda, wants her out of her mother's environment, and wants her with him. He actually may be in love with her in a sexual way; some of the imagery used to describe their departure and the extreme impatience (531) that Longdon experiences as he waits for Nanda's reply to his offer are suggestive of the would-be, if unacknowledged, lover.[13]

Much of this is left open to interpretation, of course: the reader does not know whether or not Longdon's feelings about Nanda by the end of the novel have changed from those avuncular ones that define their friendship during the earlier chapters. Nor do we know whether or not Nanda's naive, romantic desire to be kind and to think the best of people—as well as her probably unconscious desire to emulate her mother—would have led (or will lead, if she returns from Beccles) to sexual complications with the despicable Cashmore, although we do know that the relation is a threat to Nanda, seemingly a major reason Longdon wants to remove the girl from the city.

Ambiguity and the Acolytes

One result of the ambiguity in the novel is that through it James can hint at the tawdriness in Buckingham Crescent without running the risks of censorship that had plagued writers such as Émile Zola and Thomas Hardy. Another result is, as has been suggested earlier, that we as readers are placed in positions analogous to those of the characters as they attempt to puzzle out the motives of others. The reader is reminded of these facts by way of introduction to a discussion of Mitchy and Vanderbank, Mrs. Brook's two main acolytes. The former has been sentimentalized consistently by almost all critics, the latter attacked for primarily the wrong reasons. Rather than being a kind, poorly treated but sincere and pathetic little rich boy, Mitchy could just as plausibly be viewed as a weak individual, culpable in his unprincipled drifting. All we know definitely about Mitchy is that he is deeply cynical, even despairing about life, that he allows and even encourages Petherton to sponge off him, that he marries Aggie although he does not love her, that he invites Petherton on their honeymoon, and that he lingers with Nanda at the end of the novel while permitting his young wife to do what she wants with her freedom. Nanda praises Mitchy's ability to enjoy life and Longdon concludes that he is better than the others. Yet a reader may wonder how much of Mitchy's "enjoyment" derives from a somewhat sick cherishing of his own unconventionality. We may also speculate that Aggie's coming-out is somehow related to Mitchy's sexual unorthodoxy; we may therefore conclude that it was unwise for him to have married the little girl in the first place.

It is not clear why he follows Nanda's advice here. Romantic "all for Nanda" interpretations are unsatisfactory; perhaps Mitchy is simply indifferent to the institution of marriage. Nor is it clear why he hovers around Nanda at the novel's conclusion. Read positively (and sentimentally), the signs tell us of his sad devotion to Mrs. Brook's daughter; read negatively they suggest Mitchy's continuing search for unusual, prurient sensations and his obsessive need to be unconventional. (Nanda says fairly early in the novel that "It's as if he could only afford to do what's not vulgar. . . . Mitchy says 'No; I take my own line; I go in for a beggar-maid.' And it's only because I'm a beggar-maid that he wants me" [227].) However we interpret Mitchy, we should probably conclude that he is not "awkward"; he is lost.[14] Whether we will pity or condemn his behavior depends to a large extent upon our own personalities.

Critics tend to attack Van for not committing himself to a marriage with Nanda, and observe in him another example of a Jamesian Prufrock. In defense of Van one should point out that he has several understandable reasons for not marrying her: his relationship with her mother, his specific fear (which he makes obvious in the second chapter of book 4) about Nanda's undefined but disturbing friendship with Cashmore, his general fear that she is incipiently promiscuous because of her exposure to immoral people, perhaps Van's reluctance to be seen as having accepted a bribe from Longdon to marry her (although he pointedly says, "once I were disposed to act on your suggestion I'd make short work of any vulgar interpretation of my motive" [270–71]). The most important reason, however, is that, although he admires her, he does not love her, for whatever reasons. He is therefore almost terrified by her intensity and experiences cathartic relief when, during their electric, poignant meeting at Beccles, he resists the impulse to propose to her out of sympathy (344).

Not only does James suggest why it would be so difficult for Van to marry Nanda, but he also goes out of his way to reveal Van's good qualities, not simply his charisma (which, translated into modern parlance, is what the phrase often applied to Van—"sacred terror"—seems to mean). He is a competent worker, for example: he has a decent job which, unlike Edward Brookenham, he seems to have earned, and his books—an important motif in the novel—are kept in good order (cf. 126). He is kind to Mr. Longdon and tries hard to introduce him gently to the vertiginous world of Buckingham Crescent. He is sensitive enough to recognize the limitations of the world, but he can also appreciate Mrs. Brook's attempts to transform it.

Where Van is weak—unmanly, really—is in not confronting his feelings about Nanda honestly and in allowing his decisions to be made for him by the passage of time rather than by actions that he consciously performs. It is hard to know what he could have done for Nanda, but he should not have avoided her as long as he does, coming to her only after her invitation. The narrator's attitude toward Van throughout this last occasion is mordantly and devastatingly ironic, as the young man self-consciously tries to make himself feel good by letting her down easily. An early comment gives the reader a clue to the tone. In the British edition, the narrator asserts, "Vanderbank had not been in the room ten seconds before he showed that he had arrived to be kind."[15] The addition of a descriptive phrase in the New York Edition makes Van's strategy even more obvious: "Vanderbank . . . before he showed *ever so markedly* that he had arrived to be kind" (492, my italics). Then, in all versions of the text, an extremely intrusive narrative comment follows: "Kindness therefore becomes for us, by a quick turn of the glass that reflects the whole scene, the high pitch of the concert—a kindness that almost immediately filled the place, to the exclusion of anything else, with a familiar friendly voice, a brightness of good looks and good intentions, a constant though perhaps sometimes misapplied laugh, a superabundance almost of interest, inattention and movement" (492). A dimension of Van's "kindness" throughout this "concert" is his pampering of himself and his image rather than his consideration of the young person to whom he does not really listen.[16]

Also culpable is Van's failure to explain in person and to apologize to Longdon for not living up to the older person's expectations. Van's lack of manners here—and his eagerness for Nanda to cover up for him—is unequivocal evidence of his lack of courage. One wonders, finally, whether or not Van also will allow his friendship with Mrs. Brook to drift apart, despite his graceful protestations made in response to Nanda's plea that he be true to her mother. By this point we, like Mr. Longdon, should no longer trust Vanderbank, although it is

doubtful whether we will share Longdon's intensity of disgust and disillusionment. The portrait that James has drawn in Vanderbank by the
novel's conclusion is of a man who has allowed his distaste for awkwardness almost to destroy his potential for admirable behavior. Yet
even here a trace of ambiguity in the characterization remains. We
know from the following comment that Van is sufficiently sensitive to
be somewhat ashamed of his treatment of both Nanda and Mr. Longdon: "I've been a brute and I didn't mean it and I couldn't help it"
(512). Perhaps, therefore, Van will not desert Mrs. Brook despite his
embarrassment over the demands that she undoubtedly will make of
him. Perhaps he will honor his verbal vow made to Nanda. Perhaps
also when—or if—Nanda returns from Beccles, she will find her mother's circle more or less intact; or, given her mother's resilience, perhaps
there will be a new circle—and the young woman will be able to take
her place in it. Perhaps . . . but our ability to predict the future depends to a large extent on our ability to interpret character, and character in *The Awkward Age* remains ambiguous and unpredictable. One
of the paradoxical effects of the ambiguity in this in some ways most
artificial of novels, therefore, is that in this area it seems so much like
life.

Chapter Six

The Ambassadors: The Sexual Humiliation of Lambert Strether and the Idealism of Henry James

Background

Genesis and text. Writing to William Dean Howells on 9 August 1900, James lamented that his friend—and Harper editor—was uninterested in a "human, dramatic, international" and more then 100,000-word manuscript for which he had drawn up a "detailed scenario . . . a year ago, beginning then—a year ago—to do the thing—immediately afterwards."[1] This reference suggests that James had done significant work on *The Ambassadors*—the original idea for which is mentioned in an 1895 *Notebooks* entry—even before he had begun in the spring of 1900 to write *The Sacred Fount,* a novella about an observer's increasingly frantic attempts to unravel the clandestine sexual relationships between weekend visitors to an English country house. As James said in the same letter to Howells, however, he had halted for "reasons extraneous and economic."

Soon after returning in early June 1899 from his trip to the Continent, he had bought Lamb House, Rye, while retaining his lease on De Vere Gardens in London; he therefore felt the need to make money quickly. As a result, by fall 1899 he was composing either a tale or an article almost every week. In early 1900 he also began to write *The Sense of the Past* in response to a request from F. N. Doubleday, a Harper editor, for a volume of ghost stories like *The Turn of the Screw.* Then, in the spring, he began *The Sacred Fount,* which he finished in early summer. Given this literary itinerary and his usual busy social schedule, it is not surprising that, when James had time, he devoted it either to projects for which he already had a publisher or which he knew from experience he could sell quickly, rather than to a project like *The Ambassadors* about which he still had to negotiate.

In June 1900, after vacationing in London and taking the traumatic and liberating step of shaving off his beard (he had worn one for over thirty years), he returned again to *The Sense of the Past* in response to a request from Howells for an "international ghost story." It was with obvious relief, however, that James greeted Howells's 14 August letter informing him that his firm no longer needed an "international ghost." He was now free to get down to *The Ambassadors* and to develop it in his own way.

The long "Project of a Novel" (376–404) that James sent to Harper is dated 1 September 1900. During the next eight months he worked on the novel in both Rye and London, despite occasional depression and ill health, the death of Queen Victoria in January 1901, and his usual social engagements, including a lengthy visit from his brother (whose illness had been diagnosed as a heart condition) and his family. The visit culminated in William's Edinburgh lectures on "The Varieties of Religious Experience," in the winter of 1901. A little after Easter, James employed a new typist, who, unlike the previous one, William MacAlpine, could type directly from dictation. Mary Weld's first tasks were to help prepare William James's manuscript on religion for publication and to type the last chapters of his younger brother's new novel. The first nine installments of *The Ambassadors* were mailed to James's literary agent, James Pinker (whose client James had become in 1899) on 9 May 1901 and the twelfth and last installment two months later.

For unexplained reasons, James's novel did not begin to appear in serial form until early in 1903. As a result, *The Wings of the Dove,* which had been written after *The Ambassadors,* was published first. Just at the point when James's agent had recommended that his client seek a British publisher for the serial, the author learned that it had begun to appear in January 1903 in the prestigious *North American Review*—not, as he had expected, in *Harper's Monthly,* along with a laudatory essay by Howells entitled "Mr. Henry James's Later Work."

The most crucial difference between the serial and the texts later published in book form is that, in order to honor the agreement about manuscript length that he had made with Harper's, James agreed to excise three and one-half chapters from the manuscript (19, 28, 35, and a section from chapter 5). Because almost all of this material related to Chad Newsome, the young American whom Lambert Strether is sent to Paris to rescue for the family business, James thus emasculated this earliest version of his novel. The first English edition of *The Ambassadors* was published by Methuen on 24 September 1903, the first American edition by Harper's a little more than a month later,[2] and the New York Edition by Scribner's in 1909.

When the material deleted from the serial was placed back into the manuscript for the first American edition, the order of chapters 28 and 29 was reversed, either inadvertently by James himself, or by an editor, understandably misled because of James's perhaps intentionally vague transitions between chapters. Another significant error is that a line was dropped from the beginning of chapter 30 and reinserted eight lines later, thus garbling the meaning of the paragraph. Despite these problems, however, the revision was not a total disaster: three and a half chapters had been restored (albeit in not the most coherent of fashions), and James had made the kinds of stylistic improvements that he typically made between the serial and the first book editions—repeated words and commas were removed, quasi-stage directions were added, and so on.

In preparing his novel for the first English edition James had "intended to send the sheets from the corrected proofs for the first American edition to his English publishers so that they could set their edition by them" (358). Because he probably did not receive the sheets, however, despite repeated and anguished requests for them, the English edition benefited from an independent revision from James's hands. The most important difference between the English and American editions is that, in the former, chapters 28 and 29 appear in their proper order. (For other significant differences, see Rosenbaum's analysis in the Norton Critical Edition.) The biggest problem with the text is that it contains many typographical errors, most of which James himself did not notice when he marked up his own private copy.

In preparing his New York Edition of *The Ambassadors,* James for some reason revised from the Harper's text rather than the Methuen. He made many stylistic emendations; he called the large sections of the novel "books" rather than "parts" and emphasized the twelve-book structure by numbering chapters within "books," as he had done in revising *The Awkward Age,* rather than continuously throughout the novel; he also chose two frontispieces—photographs by A. L. Coburn that James entitled "By Notre Dame" and "Luxembourg Gardens." Despite James's concern for stylistic minutiae and for large architectural principles, however, he somehow failed to observe that two chapters in the Harper's text were in the wrong order: thus, the error was perpetuated. Perhaps in revising James simply saw, like most of us when we revise, what he was looking for and failed to see what he was not. The error was not reported until 1950, by a Stanford student, Robert Young.[3]

Source and influence. In his preface, James stresses the centrality to his novel of Strether's quiet exhortation—"Live all you can"—to his young friend Little Bilham in the artist Gloriani's Parisian garden. James emphasizes the sense of missed opportunities in the aging Strether's plea, as well as the question which it implies: *"Would there yet perhaps be time for reparation?"* (1).

James's source for the speech's mood of brooding melancholy is William Dean Howells, whose outpouring—provoked just as he prepared to cut short a frustratingly brief visit in Paris to his "domiciled and initiated son"—had been reported to James in late October 1895 by his young friend Jonathan Sturges, to whom the plea had been made (372–75). If one compares, moreover, Strether's exhortation in the completed novel to its source, one discovers that a significant portion of Strether's actual language derives from the original entry, not just the "thing or two" mentioned by James in his preface. Missing from the *Notebooks,* however, are any references to "the charming old garden attached to a house of art, and on a Sunday afternoon of summer, many persons of great interest being present,"—elements, James says in his preface, "which are so important in the scene" (2). In fact, if one judges from the *Notebooks,* details of setting were unimportant to Sturges, who did not even remember where he heard Howells' words. Moreover, when James first recorded the anecdote, he was not attracted to the Parisian implications of the tale about the frustrations of old age that Sturges' comments immediately began to suggest to him.

Attention is called to these facts because, when in his preface James luxuriates in memories about his source, he says, "what amplified the hint to more than the bulk of hints in general was the gift with it of the old Paris garden, for in that token were sealed up values infinitely precious" (2). Although "the old Paris garden" is important to *The Ambassadors,* this "gift" came neither from Jonathan Sturges nor from James's own imagination when he first played with the story that had been told to him. By the end of the first 1895 *Notebooks* entry, James had decided on Paris as a setting for what he assumed would be a "nouvelle," but only reluctantly. In thinking about the source more than a decade later, James misremembered, and thus engaged in nostalgic mythmaking. In this preface, James's myth is about the mysterious ease with which, and the almost magical inevitability by which, the original idea metamorphosed into *The Ambassadors*. Whatever one thinks, therefore, about the worth of this novel that came to be so deeply personal and important to its author—according to him, "the best, 'all round,'" of his works (2)—one must recognize that its relationship to its sources is not as simple as James makes out in his preface.

At the other pole, there are important elements in the novel—most notably those anticipating Strether's involvement with Chad Newsome—that James does not acknowledge in his later commentary. When James made this original lengthy notation, he was temporarily escaping from the frustrating skirmish he had engaged in with his *Spoils of Poynton* manuscript. He was losing his attempt to control its length and clearly trying to create other marketable subjects, which he might turn to if the *Spoils* project collapsed. Initially, James saw in the Howells anecdote only the impetus for one of a series of stories about old people. Its international dimension seemed relatively unimportant, even though several months before he had been asked by Harper for an international story, and then had considered ideas (recorded earlier in his *Notebooks*) as possible ways of meeting the request that, a few years later, would lead to *The Wings of the Dove* and *The Golden Bowl*. What seemed to draw him initially was the mood of regret, which James identified with old age; then, as he began to play with the idea, he found attractive a picturesque and somewhat quixotic drama deriving from a "revolution that takes place" in the consciousness of an older protagonist. James's renewal of interest in the internationalism that had earlier been his trademark came later, and only after he had explored his English environment in many tales and short novels.

No attempt will be made to trace all the steps by which this 1895 note led to *The Ambassadors*. One stage along the way, however, is worthy of some scrutiny. The stage begins in the winter of 1899 after James had finished reading proofs for *The Awkward Age* and was vacationing on the Continent; the stage ends approximately a half year later when, after a trip to the Continent, he had returned to Rye, been given a chance to buy Lamb House, and then decided to do so. During this period, as has been suggested earlier, it seems highly probable that he wrote most of the lengthy "Project of a Novel" for *The Ambassadors* and also began writing the novel itself. In Rome, for example (16 May) his notebook contains references to "Waymark" and "Newsome."[4]

Whatever the exact date upon which he began the novel, it is evident that some time during these months he had readied himself to write a book (not simply a tale) that would be significantly international and centrally about Paris.

James's imagination was undoubtedly stimulated by two visits to France made just after leaving Rye in March and before returning to it in early July. We cannot be certain whether, during his sojourns in Paris, he actually received the "gift" of the "old Paris garden" with its "values infinitely precious" that he refers to in his preface. We do know, however, that he spent a month in the city in both late spring and early summer; we know also that he was fascinated—almost awestruck—by the city during his earlier visit, upon his return for the first time in approximately five years. Writing to his architect friend Edward Warren, in late March, James exclaims about "this extraordinary Paris," this "monstrous massive flower of national decadence, the biggest temple ever built to material joys and the lust of the eyes. . . . It is a strange great phenomenon—with a deal of beauty still in its expensive symmetries and perspectives—and such a bundle of light."[5] The influence of impressionistic art that often has been noted in *The Ambassadors* is hinted at in the language of this letter. Characteristically, however, James's dominant feelings of wonder are complicated and somewhat undercut by submerged feelings of mistrust and disapproval.

In addition to this evidence of revitalized interest in the Parisian setting, there are also many suggestions in James's *Notebooks* of his renewed enthusiasm for international fiction. Even before he left Rye for the Continent, for example, he jotted down ideas that led eventually to "The Story In It," "Fordham Castle," "Mrs. Medwin," and "Flickerbridge." Then, when he was in Rome, he was told an anecdote about Julia Ward Howe that inspired "The Beldonald Holbein." Each of these tales contains significant international dimensions. James probably became receptive again to writing international fiction because, after completing *The Awkward Age,* he had grown temporarily tired of the London environment (in part, one might surmise, because his fiction about London had not brought him a larger audience). Then, when he began at Lamb House to think internationally, he created an imaginative context in which it became easy to involve himself in this kind of fictional world. On the Continent, he again met and heard about Europeanized Americans; began in Italy to research a book about the American amateur sculptor William Wetmore Story, who had lived in Italy for many years earlier in the century; and read proof for and criticized a novel (*Eleanor*) by his friend, the popular English novelist Mrs. Humphry Ward, about an American girl in Italy.

The reference to *The Awkward Age* merits elaboration. Some critics (e.g., Richards, Holland) have emphasized parallels between *The Ambassadors* and *The Sacred Fount,* the novella that James completed prior to focusing on *The Ambassadors*. The novella's relevance to *The Ambassadors* should not be minimized, even though the influence was to a certain extent negative: *The Sacred Fount* probably made James thoroughly aware of the problems inherent in narrating a long manuscript from a first-person perspective; thus, his composition of the novella may have suggested the third-person limited form of the novel, a point of view combining the intensity and immediacy of the first-person with the control and opportunity for authorial intrusion of the third.

On the other hand, the influence of *The Awkward Age* needs more recognition than it has received. If one compares the two novels, for example, one observes many resemblances: between the Woollett-Paris values conflict in *The Ambassadors* and an analogous contrast in *The Awkward Age* involving Beccles and London; between Strether's initially ambivalent attitude toward Paris and Longdon's attitude toward London; between the fascinated portrayals of Mme de Vionnet and Mrs. Brook (perhaps, as F. W. Dupee has suggested, James's portrayal of the earlier "femme du monde" gave him the confidence to portray the later one); between the Chad–Mme de Vionnet relationship and the earlier older woman–younger man relationship of Mrs. Brook and Vanderbank;[6] between the attempts of characters in each novel to force commitments upon attractive but self-centered males (in particular, the attempts of the older men to compel commitment from their younger alter egos); between the essentially sympathetic but sometimes ironic treatment of both fifty-five-year-old men. One might argue also that the response made to experience by them involves an essentially similar amalgam of the aesthetic and the moral, the open and the fixed—that complicated Jamesian value system, the "source" of which has been attributed by scholars to a variety of men: Emerson and Thoreau, William James, Walter Pater, and Matthew Arnold, for example. Whatever the source, the dramatization of Longdon's development of these values may have helped prepare James to portray an analogous change in Louis Lambert Strether.[7]

Shifting of Allegiances

More than one hundred substantial discussions of *The Ambassadors* have been written, almost all of them focusing at some point on two related topics—James's attitude toward his protagonist and the significance of the novel's puzzling ending. According to some critics, Lambert Strether's final leave-taking of two attractive women in Paris and return to anonymity in America is more or less consistent with James's earlier ironic, even satiric, treatment of the character. The majority of critics, equally certain about the mood of the novel's concluding pages and James's attitude toward his character, stress the positive significance of Strether's "renunciation": from this point of view, Strether is, for example, an existentialist hero; or a quasi-artist who eventually brings to his life "a sense of pictorial logic and a rich, compassionate tone" (Walter Wright); a comic hero who "escapes two humorous societies . . . and creates a new moral vision within his own consciousness" (Ronald Wallace); or a genuinely religious man who becomes "a disinterested witness to the truth he has arrived at" (John Warner); and so on.

Although positive responses to Strether's career are likely to correspond more closely than negative ones to the experience of most readers, nevertheless, interpretations that are too honorifically allegorical may seem unconvincing, perhaps overly sentimental to many readers, and may leave unreconciled their impression that, on the one hand, Strether's capacity for "living" in the more or less conventional sense has been augmented considerably because of his experiences in Paris; but that, on the other hand, this capacity will be diminished when Strether returns to the domain of his "blue Iceberg" (298) (Mrs. Newsome) in Woollett, Massachusetts. Such readers may feel let down—even betrayed—by the novel's ending. Philip Weinstein, whose admiration for James is severely qualified, speaks of a "hero who indicates most clearly the *narrow* beauty of his creator's vision of life" (my italics). F. O. Matthiessen illuminates the heart of the problem: "neither Strether nor his creator escapes a certain soft fussiness" (436). And Leslie Fiedler calls Strether "surely the most maidenly of all James's men."[8]

The following analysis is written primarily for readers who sense this overly ethereal "soft fussiness" and whose admiration for the novel (and perhaps for James in general) is diminished as a result. The argument will be that the longer Strether remains in Paris the more strongly sensual becomes his attraction to Marie de Vionnet; that a crucial dimension of Strether's encounter in the country with Chad and the lady is his total sexual humiliation; and that a cause of Strether's actions at the novel's conclusion is his frank, intelligent, generous, yet also partially selfish (not "disinterested") concession "to the actualities of his mind, heart, and time of life."[9] A further cause, it will be argued, is what may be called the idealism of Henry James.

James's portrayal of the process leading to his protagonist's leap from the safe but increasingly more uncomfortable protection of his New England code into the almost open boat of Marie de Vionnet is both humorous and sympathetic. Strether is cultured, imaginative, and sensually aware; at the beginning he is also insecure and sexually deprived. Mme de Vionnet is a clever, accomplished woman of refined sexuality, determined to have her own way. Given the qualities of these two characters, the evocativeness of their French environment, and the conditions in which they meet, Strether's final decision to defend Marie in the face of Mrs. Newsome's tacit, potent dismay and her daughter Sarah Pocock's overt hostility after arriving in Paris seems almost inevitable, the climax of a long rationalization.

The main stages leading to Strether's change can be listed quickly: at first, Marie is totally in the background, glimpsed dimly as the prime cause of Chad's amazing transformation into a suave gentleman; then she is partly in the foreground as the impeccable mother of the exquisite Jeanne—the gracious woman at first like (in Gloriani's garden) and then unlike (in her own evocative home) women of Strether's previous acquaintance. She moves even more into the foreground when, after a dinner at Chad's she manipulates Strether into helping discover her daughter's feelings for the young man; ten days later, when Strether recognizes Marie in Notre Dame, he persuades himself that her behavior in the church is proof of her "virtuous attachment" to Chad. The meeting also convinces him that "holding off could be but a losing game from the instant she was worked for not only by her subtlety, but by the hand of fate itself. If all the accidents were to fight on her side—and by the actual showing they loomed large—he would only give himself up" (177).

Strether's insight here about "fate" is both true and false. To his credit he is partially aware of Marie's subtlety; he is not aware, however, of the possible extent to which the "accidents" and "fate" are actually products of Marie's skill (including the meeting in Notre Dame). Nor does he recognize the limitations of his puritanical understanding of the term: in the context of this novel, "fate" does not suggest events controlled by an inscrutable Christian God, but rather decisions heavily influenced by the unconscious needs of characters themselves, in this case Strether's need to let himself go with Marie. In any event, he does "give himself up" and invites her to breakfast.

Various steps lead from the scene in Notre Dame and the restaurant on the Left Bank to Strether's declaration to Sarah: Maria Gostrey's absence, for example, and therefore Strether's opportunity to become more intimate with Marie; Marie's skill in catering subtly (unlike the unsubtle Maria) to his desire to feel masculine; his intuition that Chad may want to leave Marie; Strether's wish to benefit more obviously from a relationship that he, in all likelihood, is already being condemned for; his acute embarrassment over being identified by Marie with Maria (224) and his resulting need to assert himself in a more positive manner. At this point, the list may already seem lengthy, but there are still more steps in the subtle process worthy of observation. One notes the importance of the following events, for example: Marie's revelation that Jeanne's marriage has been arranged for, news that makes Strether feel more "intimate" with her, even though he is very disturbed; Mamie Pocock's appreciation of his Parisian friends, a response that allays his fears he may be prejudging Chad, and, by implication, Marie herself; and Strether's recognition at Chad's party that Marie is doing more for him than he for her.

Finally, there is the buffeting by Sarah Pocock in the climactically comic scene in book 10 which almost compels him to utter, "Ah dear Sarah, you must *leave* me this person here"—a statement he realizes is "perhaps the most positive declaration he had ever made in his life" (278). Soon after he decides, "And it was simple enough—it was rudimentary: not, not to give her away. 'I find in her more merits than you would probably have patience with my counting over'" (279). As has been suggested, Strether is in a sense driven to this final position; yet, even while James makes his readers aware of the large extent to which the statements are determined, he also conveys a mysterious impression of free choice here, perhaps the "illusion of freedom" (132) that Strether himself describes to Little Bilham in Gloriani's garden.

The Sexual Humiliation of Lambert Strether

In looking closely at the steps that push Strether toward these declarations, readers should observe a strong sexual dimension: as a man who in part has been made to feel inadequate, Strether has a strong need to assert himself in stereotypically "masculine" ways, a need that circumstances and Marie de Vionnet contribute to powerfully. The crucial and essentially unconscious basis (on Strether's part) of this relationship is revealed clearly in the justly famous and frequently analyzed "occasion" in the country. By the end of the scene Strether not only sees the truth about Marie and Chad's friendship (he has had glimpses of this truth before that have not affected his idealizing vision), but also feels it.

Between this epiphany and Strether's earlier defense of Marie to Sarah there are several important stages: his relationship with Mrs. Newsome has been terminated (although, characteristically, Strether qualifies his recognition of this: "all quite might be at an end. . . . It probably *was* all at an end" [280]); the gorgeous Parisian summer has made him feel excruciatingly how the youth he had lost "was an affair of the senses" (281–82); an encounter with Chad has made him more doubtful than ever about the young man's desire to remain in Paris; and a conversation with Maria Gostrey has not only allowed him to clarify his thinking about Mrs. Newsome, but, more important, has helped to build up his self-esteem. Strether leaves the meeting with his masculine ego buttressed and his emotional ties to the past temporarily ruptured. During the next few days, while Chad is mysteriously out of town, Strether visits Marie twice, now having convinced himself that he "had the right."

At the beginning of these tête-à-têtes, he asks if they could avoid discussing "anything tiresome" (304), by which he means "almost all they had hitherto talked about." Then, in luxuriating in memory over these scenes while visiting the country, he thinks, "don't be for me simply the person I've come to know through my awkward connection with Chad—was ever anything, by the way *more* awkward? Be for me, please, with all your admirable tact and trust, just whatever I may show you it's a present pleasure to me to think you?" (304–5) Strether, now almost preening, conjectures (in language subtly sexual): "It had been a large indication to meet; but if she hadn't met it what *had* she done, and how had their time together skipped along so smoothly, mild but not slow, and melting, liquefying, into his happy illusion of idleness?" Clearly, Strether the constricted Puritan has become, in some part of his consciousness, Strether the would-be lover: "He could recognize on the other hand that he had probably not been without reason, in his prior, his re-

stricted state, for keeping an eye on his liability to lapse from good
faith" (305).

It is important to observe this dimension of Strether's friendship—
and to see how he has become, albeit only semiconsciously, a sexual
rival to Chad—because the occasion ends with the older man's sexual humiliation. Prior to this, Strether's almost ludicrously confident
(although understandable) mood and the conditions coalesce to move
him inexorably to a kind of Whitmanesque transcendental experience.
Strether finds himself creating his own impressionist canvas, performing his own drama, writing his own text (306). Both the diction
and the rhythm of the narrator's language pick up the sexual over-
tones of Strether's experience: "The conditions had nowhere so asserted their difference from those of Woollett as they appeared to him
to assert it on the little court of the Cheval Blanc while he arranged
with his hostess for a comfortable climax. . . . The picture and the
play seemed to melt together in the good woman's broad sketch of
what she could do for his visitor's appetite. He felt in short a confidence, and it was general, and it was all he wanted to feel" (306).
Then, from his "small and primitive pavilion" his dream is completed as he observes an oarsman and his lady drift slowly into view:
"The air quite thickened, at their approach, with further intima-
tions; the intimation that they were expert, familiar, frequent—this
wouldn't at all events be the first time. they knew how to do it, he
vaguely felt" (307).

Strether's languid dream now becomes a nightmare, as the de Mau-
passantian (302) underside flashes into view: "It was a sharp fantastic
crisis that had popped up as if in a dream, and it had only to last the
few seconds to make him feel quite horrible" (308). The man who had
felt in the swim, in the know, receives the "odd impression of violence
averted—the violence of their having 'cut' him, out there in the eye of
nature, on the assumption that he wouldn't know it" (309). The man
who has thought himself at last fluent in French, suddenly finds it
impossible to follow Marie's "all at once little brilliant jumps" (310).
Strether's imagined "virtuous attachment" becomes "something to put
a face upon" (310); his unconscious rivalry with Chad is confronted by
evidence "that Chad in particular could let her know he left it to her"
(312); then, Strether must swallow "the deep, deep truth of the intimacy revealed" (313). Strether, who has temporarily overcome doubts
about his masculinity, is compelled to see traumatically how "he had

dressed the possibility in vagueness, *as a little girl might have dressed her doll*" (313; my italics).

Finally, the man whose conscious ruminations earlier in the scene had suggested so strongly his unconscious rivalry with Chad is compelled to perceive how "He had made them—*and by no fault of their own—momentarily pull it for him, the possibility,* out of this vagueness; and must he not therefore *take it now* as they had simply, with whatever thin attenuations, to *give it to him?*" (313; my italics). The highlighting here through italics may appear perverse to some readers. Yet what James seems to suggest, through his use of charged Victorian euphemisms, is that Strether's fantasizing has been in essence masturbatory, that he knows this, and that he temporarily feels a kind of perverse retribution. Not surprisingly, after he thinks about this experience at night in his apartment, the "question" makes Strether "feel lonely and cold" (313). Not surprisingly, in the depths of the night he finds himself "supposing innumerable and wonderful things" (313).

Strether's Grace under Pressure

As Strether's image of the little girl and the doll suggests, he not only is humiliated as a result of this encounter: he is in a significant sense emasculated. Given the probable trauma of this experience, a particular dimension of subsequent scenes is somewhat implausible— the almost unequivocally positive nature of Strether's actions during the last part of this book as he tries to set his lands in order before retiring to his New England wasteland. Sally Sears, a critic who also has observed the importance of sexuality in *The Ambassadors,* is wrong in stressing the Beckettian bleakness of the concluding chapters.[10] The point that James underlines in several valedictory scenes is that despite Strether's terrible humiliation, his fatigue, his age, and various temptations to see narrowly and act improperly or inhumanely, he acts well.

The word *act* should be emphasized here because the tendency of most critics—even those who admire Strether—is to see in him at the end an essentially passive figure. What should be stressed, therefore, is that Strether is performing a series of relatively courageous actions when he visits Marie, Chad, and Maria. Readers who compared Strether's behavior here with Vanderbank's cowardly drifting at the end of *The Awkward Age* might acknowledge this possibility. And readers who have themselves confronted a painful leave-taking should acknowledge it. Moreover, readers should also observe that, by the end of *The Am-bassadors,* James's hero is not at all concerned about the quality of life that awaits him in his bleak Arcadia: he may actually be looking forward to returning home.

When Strether agrees to visit Marie de Vionnet after the encounter in the country, he faces several temptations to treat her badly, or even to reject her. He is tempted, for example, to refuse to meet her, or to insult her subtly by meeting her in an environment not of her choosing. Strether's humiliation makes these real possibilities as does his Puritan background, which has taught him that in the case of wrongdoing someone should suffer. Either choice would cause her discomfort. During the occasion, Strether sees through Marie, notices how terribly she cares for Chad ("a man ineffably adored" [322]), discerns how exploited she has been (and risks being), and is struck by how vulgar this has made her (a shocking recognition for a man who has admired her fineness); Strether also observes her vulnerability when she breaks down.

As the scene develops, moreover, he knows that he cannot entirely trust her when she tells him she cherishes his respect—knows that she may be playing a role to manipulate him, as she had earlier. For all these reasons, his temptation is to refuse to help her. Even after he hints to her that he is prepared to offer assistance, she bitterly insults his motives: "of course, as I've said, you're acting, in your wonderful way, for yourself. . . . You'd do everything for us but be mixed up with us" (323).

Despite the contempt for herself and for Strether's fastidiousness that she evinces here, and despite his abundant and wondering sense of "the possibilities she betrayed" (323), Strether does not reject her self-recriminatory cry for help. Although he discerns painfully that she is not the perfect creature of his imagination, he maintains a full awareness of her value as a human being: "but she was as much as ever the finest and subtlest creature, the happiest apparition, it had been given him, in all his years, to meet" (323). He thus decides to help her, but not by foolishly remaining in Paris as an intermediary between Chad and her, as she would like him to do. Even when she offers what may be construed as a final sexual temptation—"we might, you and I, have been friends. . . . I've wanted you too" (324)—Strether replies generously but firmly, "Ah but you've *had* me!" He knows that he has been a pawn—in a sense, an unknowing pander—and that he wants no more of this role; yet he will still attempt to help her.

A brief scene with Maria Gostrey follows, really a prelude to the temptation she offers at the novel's conclusion. Here, Maria accuses him of dressing up "even the virtue" of Chad and Marie's relationship, and of being either "grandly cynical" or "as grandly vague" (330). Significant about Strether's reply to her criticisms is that they do not provoke him to effusive apologies or feelings of guilt: "I had phases. I had flights" (330), he admits, but he also refuses to give up his sense of the virtue in their relationship. Strether is not masochistically contrite; his response is calm and good-humored as he reveals how he has escaped the pain of his experience.

In his final scene at Chad's apartment—an encounter replete with echoes of Strether's earlier visits—the older man confronts and overcomes several temptations. It is late at night, he is very tired, and, as a result, when he intuits that "with the minimum of encouragement Chad would propose to keep him indefinitely" (334), this possibility has a brief, but potent attraction. After all, Marie de Vionnet had earlier proposed that he remain in Paris; moreover, this act could cater to Strether's drive to be consistent. The reader is not told why Strether does not succumb here. What seems to happen, however, is that merely by opening his mouth and explaining his errand, he is able to move beyond the thought of a life of comfort in Paris and the probability of a role as a buffer for Chad as he eases away from Marie and toward a return to America.

This scene has several other noteworthy aspects. One is Strether's ability to see through Chad, just as he had done in his earlier meeting with Chad's mistress. Because of his prescience, Strether is able to choose arguments that should have maximum impact. At first he tries appealing to Chad's utilitarian principles: "I feel how much more she can do for you. She hasn't done it all yet" (337). Strether quickly understands, however, that this argument is not going to work: "He meant no harm, though he might after all be capable of much; yet he spoke of being 'tired' of her almost as he might have spoken of being tired of roast mutton for dinner" (337). As a result, Strether combines his utilitarian argument with a direct appeal to Chad's New England sense of duty: "You owe her everything—very much more than she can ever owe you" (338).

Finally, near the end of the scene, after Chad begins to discuss the marvels of advertising, Strether feels as if the young man "had begun to dance a fancy step," feels also "a little faint" (339) when he immediately deciphers Chad's strategy, and then appeals even more forcefully to a nonmaterialistic principle: "Oh damn the money in it! . . . Shall you give your friend up for the money in it?" (340). Chad protests that he cannot be bribed, and pretends to kick the bribe away. But Strether remains undeceived: "You're restless" (340). Throughout the occasion Chad uses all of his charm to, in essence, try to convince Strether to condone whatever he, Chad, chooses to do. But Strether understands the young man's strategy and does what he can to pin responsibility onto him. "What he can" is the significant idea here: Strether is not the least bit optimistic, but he does his best under the circumstances.

There is one other observation worth making about Strether's behavior: despite his very large emotional investment in Chad,[11] and despite the evidence of Chad's desire to escape responsibility, Strether is not disillusioned and tries to give him his due. This fact is mentioned because of the tendency of some critics to see in Chad at the end a villain exposed. Strether's vision of his friend is clearer, more imaginatively sympathetic, and more humane: Chad, within limits, is kind and concerned, but he is also younger than his mistress, lacks Strether's sympathetic imagination, is restless and ambitious (now that he has been made fully aware of his potential value), and wants to go home. As Strether has noted earlier with some regret but also equanimity, despite all Marie and his own "high appreciation" have done for the young man, "he was none the less only Chad. . . . The work, however admirable, was nevertheless of the strict human order" (332). In all probability, therefore, Chad eventually will leave his mistress (he already may have another woman friend in London), show how he "is the son of his father!" (341), and become a success in advertising. Perhaps from a certain perspective these actions will make him a callous monster, but the perspective seems not to be that of Henry James.

Point of View in the Novel

As a preliminary to a reading of the frequently analyzed last scene of *The Ambassadors*, a topic will now be discussed whose relevance to an understanding of this occasion should become obvious—James's handling of "point of view." At this stage in the history of James criticism, there are probably few serious readers who accept without large qualifications the theory first advanced by the master himself that, in the novel, for purposes of unity and intensity, he employed "but one centre and [kept] it all within my heroe's compass. The thing was to be so much this worthy's intimate adventure that . . . his consciousness [was projected] upon it from beginning to end without intermission or deviation" (8). James as narrator certainly does not separate his perspective from that of the primary point-of-view character as frequently as he had in earlier long novels such as *The Tragic Muse,* nor to the extent that nineteenth-century creators of "loose baggy monsters" were in the habit of doing. It needs to be stressed, however, that there are many instances in which James as narrator does "intrude," in various ways, when there are particular effects to be achieved by so doing.[12]

Some intrusions are merely narrative tags designed to remind the reader that Strether is to be observed as well as identified with, and, at the same time, to encourage a certain warm relationship with the protagonist: thus, he is often referred to as "our friend" (e.g., 121), or, less frequently, "poor Strether" (e.g., 148). A less obvious, more ambiguous type of "intrusion" is exemplified in the imagery of certain pictorial passages. One example derives from Strether's sense of the contrast between his relationship with Chad and his mistress after the scene in the countryside, and his continuing friendship with Maria Gostrey: "These others appeared to him now horribly complex; they bristled with fine points, points all unimaginable beforehand, points that pricked and drew blood; a fact that gave to an hour with his present friend . . . something of the innocent pleasure of handling rounded ivory" (326). Strether may be capable of the quasi-metaphysical imagery here, but, more plausibly, although the perception is Strether's, the mode of expression is the narrator's, as he intrudes to clarify and vivify a contrast Strether feels strongly. When James wants us to see the perception and language as belonging to his hero, he usually makes this clear. Thus, "They now took on to his fancy, Miss Gostrey and he, the image of the Babes in the Woods"; earlier, Strether imagines resemblances between Mme de Vionnet and "Madame Roland" (317), and Marie and "Cleopatra in the play, indeed various and multifold" (160).

Another somewhat ambiguous type of what might be called narrative "intrusions" are the many instances in which particular perceptions or interpretations sound authorial, but that may belong to Strether. As Strether nerves himself to meet Chad, for example, after the "adventure" (326) in the countryside, the older man tries to prepare himself to act for the right reasons, not because "he was sore or sorry or impoverished, because he was maltreated or desperate." The passage concludes, "It would have sickened him to feel vindictive" (327). At this

point, Strether may or may not be able to predict his own visceral
response to future immoral behavior; the comment, therefore, may or
may not be authorial.[13] But here it does not matter: the reader should
be impressed by the idealistic conviction whether it comes directly
from Strether or from the narrator; the effect is therefore the same.

There are many examples of interpretive comments that seem definitely authorial—relatively unequivocal instances of the narrator's "violation" of Strether's point of view. In the chapter, for example, in
which Strether surprises Mamie Pocock on the balcony, the narrator
observes, "He was doubtless not to know till afterwards, on turning
them over in thought, of how many elements his impression was composed" (247). This tendency of the narrator, by the way, to shift his
camera forward occurs often, as James stresses which particular moments are crucial to Strether, suggests the amount of time Strether
spends in interpreting these moments, and, more generally, suggests
the extent to which any definition of "experience" must include not
only events in space and time, but also the individual's subsequent
ruminations about them.

Still other types of authorial manipulations of point of view (not
exactly "intrusions," but nonetheless deviations from the norm) are
worth mentioning. There are the instances, for example, when in
pictorial sections of the novel James refuses to take his camera inside
Strether's consciousness: thus, for reasons of suspense, after Strether
receives his long awaited and dreaded letter from Mrs. Newsome
near the middle of the novel, the reader is denied access to Strether's
mind; instead, we see Strether crumpling paper and compressing
it in his fist (182). Such examples might be labeled "intrusive non-
intrusions." Another type of "intrusion" are the quasi-stage directions during scenic sections: "Little Bilham's eyes rested on him a
moment with some intensity; then suddenly, as if everything had
cleared up, he gave a happy laugh" (259); "'I see. They quarrel,' said
Chad rather comfortably, 'with *us*.' Strether noted once more the
comfort" (286).

In examples like these, the semiotic evidence made available to the
reader through the narrator seems also to have been observed by
Strether. In several instances, however, it is questionable whether or
not Strether would perceive what the narrator's comments allow the
reader to observe. In Strether's tense and moving final meeting with
Marie, for example, when she does all she can to persuade him to
remain in Paris, the narrator follows one of her statements with the

tag, "she nervously repeated" (321). If Strether misses this nervousness, then perhaps James is trying to allow us to be slightly ahead of his protagonist in perceiving Marie's desperate attempt to maintain control, an attempt that soon breaks down totally. A less ambiguous example is from the penultimate scene with Maria Gostrey: "What now lingered in poor Maria's face was the somewhat smoky light of the scene between them [Strether and Mme de Vionnet]. If the light however wasn't, as we have hinted, the glow of joy, the reasons for this also were perhaps discernible to Strether even through the blur cast over them by his natural modesty" (328–29).

In a passage like this in which the narrator becomes so obviously "intrusive," there is crucial information James does not want his primary method to prevent him from giving: the narrator goes on to comment about Maria's motives and her frustration in being no closer to Strether after his experience in the country than she had been earlier. Although the reasons for Maria's sadness are only "perhaps discernible to Strether," they are sufficiently important to be clarified for the reader by the narrator.

It should be emphasized that several times the narrator does not merely provide suggestive stage directions to his reader; he actually interprets the thoughts and motives of characters other than Strether: "Picking up a hat in the vestibule he [Chad] came out with his friend, came downstairs, took his arm, affectionately, as to help and guide him, treating him if not exactly as aged and infirm, yet as a noble eccentric who appealed to tenderness" (338). Chad's kind but slightly patronizing attitude here suggests that Strether may be wise in deciding not to remain in Paris with the young man. Two other examples of this type of "intrusion" are worth observing: "Miss Gostrey but desired to help his lucidity. She had however to be light and tactful" (192); "She [Maria] considered him with one of her deep returns of indulgence—returns out of all proportion to the irritations they flooded over" (330). It is authorial comments like these, along with statements made by Maria herself, that help—particularly in the last part of *The Ambassadors*—to round out and redeem James's characterization of Maria. She is not always so foolishly indulgent with Strether as she often appears to be. She is, for example occasionally irritated by his refusal to feel resentment against her friend and rival Marie de Vionnet, and exasperated by his saintliness. Such responses, moreover, help to complicate James's portrayal of Strether's ethical behavior at the end of the novel.

The Last Chapter of *The Ambassadors*

James has a difficult task in the last chapter of *The Ambassadors*. One intended function of Maria's affection has been to convince the reader of Strether's value. James knows, however, that for several reasons (as critics have displayed their ingenuity in pointing out) his hero must leave Maria and return to America. The most important reason is that he does not love her. Whether or not he is still infatuated with Marie de Vionnet is open to question. A related reason is that, as James says in his "Project of a Novel," "He has come so far through his total little experience that he has come out on the other side—on the other side, even, of a union with Miss Gostrey" (403). Other factors may also influence Strether's decision: his earlier resentment at being linked with her (his pride does not want to provide justification for Victorian equivalents of "I told you so"); his knowledge that he could not be comfortable in Paris, in part because the environment is too sensual, in part because he is tired of discerning only "what things resemble" (126) rather than what they are;[14] his strong fatalistic sense that his adventure is linked to a pattern that can only be completed if he returns home; and so on. In sum, Strether must leave.

Yet, if Strether appears to have dropped Maria too unceremoniously, the picture of his exemplary behavior that James has been sketching will be marred—and Strether will seem too much like Chad—and the essentially optimistic tone of the novel will be blurred. That James was a bit uncomfortable with the ending is suggested in the preface to the New York Edition by his somewhat dismissive comments about Maria as merely a "ficelle" (or functional character) (12): James protests too much. And of course many readers have read pessimism and/or antiheroism into this final chapter. Given the task James had set for himself, however, probably nothing he could have done would have established for some readers either the image of his protagonist or the tone he desired to create.

By the end of *The Ambassadors*, James wants us to recognize that Strether's experience has educated his consciousness. Earlier, his imagination enables him to view positively both his environment and characters whom he meets. Unlike Mrs. Newsome, he finds it extremely difficult to imagine "stupidly," "meanly": he cannot really imagine "horrors" (299). The weakness of this habit of mind is that it allows him to be deceived, to romanticize, to overvalue events and people. Although his experience in the country shatters his illusions, he has not been made cynical by the episode, as his subsequent generosity to Chad and Marie suggests. He has maintained a marvelous capacity to empathize with persons and the environment; yet, at the same time, he has learned about his tendency to dress up virtue, and he knows that places and people may be deceptive. By the time of his last visit to Maria, Strether has learned how to act not only sympathetically but wisely. As a reader of texts (to use an image that James himself employs), Strether can now qualify sympathy with judgment.

At the beginning of this final occasion, Strether's empathetic imagination is strongly present: "the place had never before struck him as so sacred to pleasant knowledge, to intimate charm, to antique order, to neatness that was almost august" (340). This perception is undeniably Strether's, but the manner of expression is authorial, as through the diction and balanced phrases the narrator emphasizes the potent appeal of the setting to Strether's consciousness. "Strether's [eyes] were comforted at all events now" (340). The insight here sounds authorial: Strether probably could not intellectualize this effect of the scene. In it, "our friend resignedly expressed himself. He spoke even with a certain philosophic humour" (341). These comments sound authorial, and not simply because of the phrase "our friend." Although Strether probably cannot articulate his mood, the mood must be identified: Strether does not want to do what he knows he must do, but he will perform this mandatory action calmly.

Strether informs Maria that he plans to leave, and she, with decorous desperation, seizes a phrase used by him (her home is a "haunt of ancient peace") and tries to turn it to her advantage: "I wish with all my heart . . . I could make you trust it as a haven of rest." Stage directions follow this blatant appeal: "On which they fronted each other, across the table, as if things unuttered were in the air." James wants this scene to be obviously dramatic, and he resorts to unsubtle Victorian narrative technique to guarantee that it will be. "Strether seemed, in his way, when he next spoke, to take some of this up" (341). Reference has been made to James's occasional refusal to penetrate Strether's mind at points when it has been the author's custom to do so. Here we remain outside Strether's consciousness not only for suspense, but also to encourage us to ponder Strether's motives.

The analysis of the remainder of this occasion will move more quickly, the purpose in selecting particular examples being to suggest how James through various means attempts to be both honest about Maria's frustration and, at the same time, supportive of Strether's decision. The narrator observes that, in thinking over Maria's comments, Strether "brooded there opposite to her, but without gloom" (341). James's hero offers to identify the hitherto unnamed Woollett object, but "She had done with the products of Woollett for all the good she had got from them" (342). Since at this point the narrator is summarizing dialogue, Maria may actually have said this (although the overt bitterness is uncharacteristic). Whether she did or not, however, her frustration has been conveyed to the reader.

The narrator describes Strether as observing Maria "kindly but attentively" (342). In response to her prediction that Chad will eventually leave Marie, Strether "waited a moment . . . pleading with her in various suggestive and unspoken ways for patience and understanding" (342). Strether tells Maria honestly that his relationship with Mrs. Newsome is over, and Maria is "satisfied and gratified" to be so informed. Strether "was affected in advance by what he believed might come from her, and he would have liked to forestall it and deal with it tenderly; yet in the presence of it he wished still more to be—though as smoothly as possible—deterrent and conclusive" (343). Some of these examples are clear instances of narrative "intrusions," some are only arguably so. Each, however, suggests that Strether is searching for a way to do humanely what he feels he must do, even though he suspects that his strategy with Chad will not prevent the young man from eventually leaving his mistress.

Almost everything that Strether says and does in the last part of the occasion communicates his kindness, his resolution, and his control. What is also suggested strongly is that he does not want to act too quickly, because he has learned from Marie de Vionnet the value of "making deception right." Finally, "He had got it at last" (344). At this point, he seems to have discovered the argument that will help him best achieve his purpose: he now launches his explanation about his need to be "right" and his desire to garner, through his experience, nothing for himself. Since Strether is so obviously trying to find throughout this meeting a generous way of extricating himself from a relationship no longer possible for him, the reader cannot be certain whether or not Strether means what he says here. Probably his creator himself does not know.

The reader should know, however, through the following comments made by the "intrusive" narrator, that Strether's argument works: "Honest and fine, she couldn't greatly pretend she didn't see it. Still she could pretend just a little" (345). Immediately, the exaggerated, essentially jocular tone of their previous conversations is reestablished: "'It isn't so much your *being* "right"—it's your horrible sharp eye for what makes you so. . . .' She sighed it at last all comically, all tragically, away. 'I can't indeed resist you.' 'Then there we are!' said Strether" (345). Maria has not been crushed; her wit and pride are intact; she will get over the jilting. So too will Strether, as he rejects Maria's well-intentioned but somewhat demeaning vision "of lightened care, for the rest of his days" and returns to America where, "There will always be something. . . . A great difference—no doubt. Yet I shall see what I can make of it" (344).

As much as F. O. Matthiessen admired James and this novel, he felt compelled to write, "The burden of *The Ambassadors* is that Strether has awakened to a wholly new sense of life. Yet he does nothing at all to fulfill that sense. Therefore, fond as James is of him, we cannot help feel his relative emptiness" (436). Here Matthiessen is wrong. It is a mistake to be disappointed by the ending of *The Ambassadors* or to read it pessimistically. Although all is not for the best in the best of all worlds, Strether is not empty: he is full of possibility. And although he will not always be right or successful, when he returns to America he will continue to do what he can—for others and for himself.

Chapter Seven
The Wings of the Dove: James's Loose, Baggy Monster
Background

Genesis and text.   James's first references to the ideas that eventually led to *The Wings of the Dove* appear in two November 1894 *Notebooks* entries. After his failure in the theater with the *Guy Domville* debacle in January 1895, however, he did not turn to these ideas again for several years, probably some time during the late winter or early spring of 1899, when, after finishing *The Awkward Age,* he was visiting France and Italy. By the fall of that year, several letters to his agent, James Pinker, suggest that James already had written a synopsis for the novel and was eager for Pinker to arrange serialization (eight serial episodes of 10,000 words each) with an American publisher. Although Pinker tried to comply, by May 1900 James seems to have accepted the failure of serialization. Yet references in his 9/14 August letter to William Dean Howells suggest that he had begun the novel, and by mid-October Pinker had made arrangements for it to be published simultaneously by Archibald Constable in England and Scribner's in the United States. James's deadline for delivery of the manuscript was 1 September 1901, a deadline he was confident of meeting because at this point he was well under way with his work on *The Ambassadors* and believed that, after completing it, he would have several months to write the new novel, as yet unnamed.

Because of problems in finishing *The Ambassadors,* however, James did not begin to dictate the new novel until 9 July 1901, and as a result requested an extension until the end of the year. Writing to Pinker on 6 November, he spoke confidently about his progress, about his plans to complete a volume of short stories while in London during the winter (*The Better Sort* was not published until 1903), and about his desire to sign a contract for another novel. Despite his confidence, James did not meet this new deadline. By the time he had moved to

London in late January 1902, he had written approximately seven and one half books, and was apparently hoping to complete the remaining books while reading proof for the ones already written. Unfortunately, almost immediately upon arriving, he became ill, an illness perhaps in part provoked by the stress of writing the sections of the novel dealing with Milly Theale's death.

Even after returning prematurely to Rye in mid-February he continued to have problems with his health. As a result, he was compelled to delay his completion of the novel, by this point with an anticipated July publishing date. Even though James finished the book in late May, however, *The Wings of the Dove* was not published until the end of August 1902, primarily, it seems, because of his failure again to meet his publisher's deadlines—this time for the providing of proofs. Viewed initially as a short novel that would be relatively simple to write, and begun confidently, *The Wings of the Dove* was completed as a lengthy work written under increasing duress and recriminations between author and publishers. James's dominant feelings upon finishing seem to have been relief and embarrassment, because of the novel's excessive length.[1]

There are three versions of the text of *The Wings of the Dove*: the English (of 4,000 copies) and American (of 3,000) editions, published within one day of each other in late August 1902, and the New York Edition published in 1909. The editors of the excellent Norton Critical Edition of *The Wings of the Dove*, Donald Crowley and Richard Hocks, argue convincingly for the superiority of the Scribner's two-volume edition over the Constable one-volume edition. Their conclusion is that "James sought to revise substantially the proof sheets for the American text while only correcting obvious errors for Constable" (411).[2] There are also more than one thousand substantive differences between the earlier texts and the New York Edition, and the total number is significant, even though most of the revisions involve only "slight shifts in word order, the omission of commas and pronouns, and the use of contractions" (416).

Source and influence. James writes in the first *Notebooks* entries related to *The Wings of the Dove* (3 and 7 November 1894), "Isn't perhaps something to be made of the idea that came to me some time ago . . . the little idea of the situation of some young creature (it seems to me preferably a woman, but of this I'm not sure), who, at 20, on the threshold of a life that seemed boundless, is suddenly condemned to death (by consumption, heart-disease, or whatever) by the voice of the physician?" As James's imagination embroiders this "little idea" (probably intended to provoke a short story), he eventually sees in it a possible three-act play. Many elements appearing in the entries antic- ipate, in a fashion, aspects of the novel: a rich young woman, for ex- ample, resenting and clawing against her doom; a poor young man unable to marry an "elder girl," who encourages him to play up to the dying heroine; the young man's revulsion against his fiancée and love for the dead girl. An alternative ending considered by James, "in the case of a play that one might entertain any hope of having acted," would have the hero "buy off" the fiancée with the money before the girl's death; then, he "would go back to the poor girl as her very own. Under this delight she would revive and cleave to him, and the curtain would fall on their embrace, as it were, and the *possibility* of their marriage and of her living" (451).

In view of the disparity between this claptrap and the novel even- tually written, it may seem inaccurate to observe in these early entries any meaningful particular "source" for *The Wings of the Dove*. The origin of the entries seems to have been that part of James's personality that yearned to succeed in the theater and which found almost viscerally appealing, despite his occasional irony and contempt, melodramatic characters and conflicts as long as they could be purged of their most blatant elements. Certainly in these entries there are prefigurements of the novel. What at first glance seems to be missing from the *Notebooks*, however, is any hint of the novel's subsequent greatness: the complex- ity of characterization, the profundity of the themes, the power and mystery deriving from the peculiar, sinuous structure, and the evoca- tiveness of the richly imagined settings. What does remain, however, as critics such as Peter Brooks have explained, is a possible emotive power, which James can call into being because of the links of his basic situation to the rawness of melodrama.

When one considers the nature of these *Notebooks* entries, one might argue that another important "source" of *The Wings of the Dove* was James's failure in the theater, because it liberated him from dramatiz- ing these ideas too quickly and in the wrong medium. As a result, he gained time to learn more about life and art; he also gained the desire and confidence to apply this knowledge appropriately. Rather than writing the embarrassingly inept and melodramatic play that the *Note- books* entries seemed to anticipate, James prepared to risk the large, great, subtle novel *The Wings of the Dove* unequivocally is.

There are, of course, other particular sources of the novel that should be noted. Scholars who have been fascinated by the luminous title character and the novel's examination of the complex interrelationship between the physical and psychological in the process of her death have suggested as possible sources James's sister Alice (who, after a time, did not want to live); his admiring friend, the writer and probable suicide Constance Fenimore Woolson; James's father (who seemed to will his own death approximately eleven months after that of his wife in late January 1882); and, in particular, the writer's beloved cousin.[5] Writing of Minny Temple in *Notes of a Son and Brother,* the second volume of his autobiography, James asserts, "she would have given anything to live—and the image of this, which was long to remain with me, appeared so the essence of tragedy that I was in the far-off aftertime to seek to lay the ghost by wrapping it, a particular occasion aiding, in the beauty and dignity of art" (471). James's thoughts about each of these people—in particular Minny Temple—undoubtedly influenced *The Wings of the Dove,* as, probably, did his failure in the theater. Here, in his own experience, he was pushed toward a kind of death while desiring to live.

Important also to these dimensions of the novel were his visit to Italy in 1899 and his renewed interest in international fiction. In Venice he visited the Daniel Curtises at the Palazzo Barbaro, the undoubted model for Milly Theale's sumptuous retreat. Of Venice itself, James wrote: "one clings, even in the face of the colder stare, to one's prized Venetian privilege of making the sense of doom and decay a part of every impression. . . . What was most beautiful is gone; what was next most beautiful is, thank goodness, going" (463). It was also during his sojourn in Italy that James read proofs of Mrs. Humphry Ward's *Eleanor,* complained about her treatment in the novel of the American girl, Lucy Foster, criticized Mrs. Ward for not making the two main female characters sufficiently antithetical, and told his friend of his desire to "rewrite" the book. What is being suggested here is not that there is a direct relationship between James's impressions of Venice, his response to *Eleanor,* and *The Wings of the Dove,* but that the collocation of these experiences helped to move James toward a conception of his central character (the girl in the *Notebooks* entries is not an "American girl") in a particular setting, one unusually evocative of doomed beauty and the mingling of material and spiritual.

At least as important as James's memories of individual people and his experience in Italy in influencing his creation of Milly and the manner of her dying is James's attitude toward the character and his conception of the novel as a whole. Many critics have discerned in Milly at once a particular, successfully individualized young person—an "American girl" reminiscent of earlier Jamesian characters such as Daisy Miller and Isabel Archer—and an almost archetypal figure suggestive, for example, of Dante's Beatrice, several of Shakespeare's heroines, and Christ.[4] Admirers of the novel as a whole have also seen in it a peculiar but powerful and resonant combination of Balzacian novel of intrigue, Howellsian novel of manners, and Hawthornian romance, at times suggestive in its texture and scope of epic poetry and Shakespearean drama, anticipating in its combination of detail and controlled symbolism novels such as Joyce's *Ulysses*.[5]

Whatever one thinks about such praise, one must recognize that James's eventual—perhaps not clearly understood—intention was to write in *The Wings of the Dove* an important and complex book. In all probability, writing *The Ambassadors* encouraged him (at least subconsciously) to try, in his new work, to create an international novel even richer and more ambitious than the one he had just completed. Because of this attitude, James could see in his potential sources possibilities he obviously did not intuit—that in fact he was incapable of intuiting—when he made his initial entries in November 1894.

The significance of James's change in attitude is even more patent in the characterization of Kate Croy. Some critics have observed in Kate hints of Alice James's nurse, Katharine Loring, or of Henry's aunt. Others have noted links between Kate Croy and earlier Jamesian creations—minor ones such as Kate Theory of "Georgina's Reasons" or Rose Arminger of *The Other House,* and major ones such as Isabel Archer (because she too refuses to compromise with life), even Olive Chancellor of *The Bostonians* (because of Kate's possible lesbian tendencies). Most frequently and persuasively, however, critics have seen in Kate analogies to literary creations such as Lady Macbeth and other figures of Jacobean tragedy, Thackeray's Becky Sharpe, and Ibsen's "bad heroines" (most plausibly Hedda Gabler); there are even aspects of James's treatment of Kate that may remind the reader of Milton's Satan. Yet, although each of these possible sources (except for Rose Arminger) was potentially available in the fall of 1894, the original references to the Kate Croy figure suggest only a simplistically conceived melodramatic villainess. Whatever one thinks of Kate Croy's actions in *The Wings of the Dove,* on the other hand, one must observe her large dimensions. Moreover, she is in some respects an artist; as well, she exhibits an almost Nietszchian quality in her drive to escape genteel poverty and to dominate her upper-middle-class milieu, the Darwinian implications of which James had been exploring for a number of years. James's source for the character of Merton Denscher is at once simple and difficult to recognize. In the original *Notebooks* entry, he is a young man of refined sensibilities and sympathetic imagination, a type whose personality more or less resembles that of his creator, and who appears repeatedly in James's fiction from the beginning of his career. In the *Notebooks*, the actions of this Ur-Denscher are cloyingly noble; moreover, James's attitude toward him and his renunciatory gesture is embarrassingly sentimental. In *The Wings of the Dove*, however, as will be argued later, both the character and his creator's attitudes toward him are considerably more complicated. Between the entry and the novel, James dramatized new and interesting variations of the type—Sir Claude (*What Maisie Knew*) and Vanderbank (*The Awkward Age*), for example. James also portrayed several individuals respectful of or fixated on the dead—for example, George Stransom ("The Altar of the Dead"), Marmaduke ("Maud Evelyn"), and Longdon (*The Awkward Age*). Although a few critics have observed in Denscher the same types of literary sources and analogues that have obviously influenced James's conceptions of Milly and Kate, the most plausible sources for the character are in James's own personality and fiction—although, as Leon Edel suggests, there is probably in Denscher something of James's young bisexual friend, the Parisianized journalist Morton Fullerton. As far as Denscher's quasi-spiritual angst and the quasi-religious conversion experienced by him are concerned, one must see a possible source in James's reflections on his brother's magnificent *The Varieties of Religious Experience*. Although the book was published in the same year as *The Wings of the Dove*, William James lived with his brother, and dictated the University of Edinburgh Gifford lectures to his brother's secretary, during the period when Henry was finishing *The Ambassadors* and preparing to begin *The Wings of the Dove*. Lecture 8, "The Divided Self, and the Process of its Unification," may be particularly relevant as a gloss on Denscher's situation.

James's Preface to the Novel

James's preface to the New York Edition of *The Wings of the Dove* contains a great deal of provocative theoretical material, including his influential discussion of the reader of fiction's need for "attention of perusal" (14–15). Yet, probably the most interesting aspect of the pre-

face is James's obvious unease in discussing his novel. Everywhere there
is evidence of ambivalence. In explaining the subject of *The Wings of
the Dove,* for example, James begins by discussing how it focuses on
Milly Theale; then, in examining Kate Croy and Merton Denscher,
and the manner in which their relation was intended to subserve the
predicament of the heroine, James implies that his interest in this "far
from a common couple" (14) makes them part of a complex—now no
longer unified—subject. In referring to other dimensions of his novel,
James openly laments the "absent values, the palpable voids, the missing links, the mocking shadows, that reflect, taken together, the early
bloom of one's good faith" (9).

As James comments on the specifics of the novel, his preface at times
reads like a litany of failure, despite occasional evidence of pride in
accomplishment. His problem in dealing with *The Wings of the Dove* is
that examples are everywhere in it of the disparity between conscious
intention and actual achievement. So too is evidence that James's own
canons of excellence—particularly the shibboleth of unity—are constantly being violated. What has happened is that, having suggested
the limitations of "loose, baggy monsters" in the preface to *The Tragic
Muse,* James is compelled in his discussion of the later novel to rationalize his own example of the type.

To James's immense credit, however, despite the seductiveness of his
self-image as controlled artist and his reluctance to be iconoclastic,
there are times in the preface when he admits perplexity about the
narrative: "He [the artist] places, after an earnest survey, the piers of
his bridge—he has at least sounded deep enough, heaven knows, for
their brave position; yet the bridge spans the stream, after the fact, in
apparently complete independence of these properties, the principal
grace of the original design" (9). Characteristically, however, he cush-
ions the shock of this admission by pointing out that "Such cases are
for him abnormal."

Yet, with respect to *The Wings of the Dove,* the "bridge" does span
the stream: James's "baggy monster" is a great novel, to a significant
degree because it is "loose" by Jamesian standards. The work fortunately lacks a truly unified subject: because he trusts his intuition
about the intrinsic importance and value of Kate Croy and Merton
Denscher, James allows his dramatization of the couple's relation and
their individual personalities to explode the single subject. He thus
adds immensely to the richness of the novel. Milly Theale, of course,
maintains significance in that, like Isabel Archer, she continues to af-

front her destiny (albeit indirectly, opaquely, and mysteriously). But unlike Isabel, she is not surrounded by essentially flat and two-dimensional characters. The diverse ways in which critics have responded to each of James's protagonists in *The Wings of the Dove* help prove his success in creating a provisional and multifarious reality for them.

A concomitant sign of the novel's relative "looseness" is the continual impression conveyed to the reader that, when James allows himself to spin out the logic of his characters and their sinister predicament, he frequently creates situations in which his ability to respond, interpret, or judge is subverted. What is being suggested here is not the commonplace that, in many instances, James is being "intentionally ambiguous": his response is frequently less cerebral than this. A sense of puzzlement, of mystery, pervades this novel, wonderfully appropriate, one comes to feel, for a work in which characters are immersed in "some pool of a Lorelei . . . [in] strange difficulties and still stranger opportunities," and are "confronted with rare questions and called upon for new discriminations" (5). Because *The Wings of the Dove* raises so many questions about human behavior and destiny that the author himself seems unable to answer, the reader may be involved in a way unlike his involvement with any other James novels, despite their epistemological uncertainties. In some of James's puzzle fiction—*The Turn of the Screw* and *The Sacred Fount* for example—a reader may feel (as in some contemporary metafiction) that he is being teased by the author, that he is part of a somewhat willful game in which only James knows the rules. Here, however, it is almost as if he needs help, and asks for it.

Situation Ethics

Consider the last chapter of book 6, an "occasion" that begins with Denscher visiting Milly at her London hotel and ends with him preparing to drive her carriage for an afternoon ride, after Kate, who enters while Milly is dressing for the ride, decides to leave without seeing her, so that Denscher may pursue his strategic friendship with the young American. Prior to the visit, Aunt Maud breathes to Denscher that "I *can*—I can smooth your path. She's charming, she's clever, and she's good. And her fortune's a real fortune" (223). The fact that Aunt Maud "believed him bribable" troubles him greatly, and his unease sporadically assaults him during his interview with Milly. At times, his reasons for visiting seem specious, she likes him, and he does not wish to lead her on. His problem becomes severe when Milly asks him to drive her carriage because he knows—almost occultly—that, if he does, a casual acquaintance will become more intimate. Denscher watches himself preparing to plunge into dangerous waters and, since we view the scene from his perspective, we share his suspense and malaise. By almost compelling the reader to share, interpret, and evaluate Denscher's adventure as it unfolds moment by moment, James also creates an extremely complicated and unsettling experience.

Viewed simplistically, the reader observes a long process of rationalization at the end of which Denscher permits himself to perform an action that is at best misleading, at worst morally contemptible. Yet early in the chapter, even while allowing us to understand why it is to Denscher's psychic advantage to invent pious motives for befriending Milly, and even while enabling us to observe the young man actually almost deluding himself, James simultaneously suggests another reading. Having considered, for example, that a potential response to the "irrational, exorbitant" appeal of Kate and her pushy aunt would be not to visit Milly, Denscher's "bewildered view" had "cleared itself up" into a conclusion that, since common courtesy requires him to visit Milly and since other people are promoting the visit, "he should surely be rather a muff not to manage by one turn or another to escape disobliging" (225). Because at the same time Denscher is congratulating himself for his "own good sense and good humour" (224) and has concluded that "He had never known himself so generally merciful" (225), we recognize his strategy here for making himself feel good. Yet Denscher's conscious reasons for visiting are not totally spurious; moreover, it is only in retrospect that we discern the terrible irony in the comment that "Should he find he couldn't work it there would still be time enough" (225).

As Denscher and Milly converse, he discerns that a reason for her interest is his ostensible need for sympathy: she thinks that Kate does not love him. He is aware also that he likes Milly and now asks himself whether "he might soon pretend to the grievance in order not to miss the sweet?" He then thinks that, thus far, only Kate has lied; he has "done nothing deceptive." Yet his conscience is sufficiently subtle to know that it might be hard to distinguish between "acting and not acting," and "He saw it with a certain alarm rise before him that everything was acting that was not speaking the particular word." Denscher rises to this challenge by reasoning that it would be "indelicate" to tell the truth about his relation with Kate; moreover, "Kate's design was something so extraordinarily special to Kate that he felt himself shrink from the complications involved in judging it"; also, "Loyalty was of course supremely prescribed in presence of any design on her part, however roundabout, to do one nothing but good" (228).

It is as convenient for Denscher to "shrink" from judging Kate as it is to conclude that loyalty is "supremely prescribed" and that Kate's "design" should do "nothing but good." Nonetheless, his conclusions have some cogency: James and the reader can observe the process of rationalization, and yet not be certain how to judge it. Occasionally, James treats his young man with devastating irony, mostly notably after Eugenio has denied him entrance to Milly's palace, and while roaming Venice, Denscher alternates between hating Lord Mark and lamenting that a man of his own "parts" must experience "a smack of the abject" (330). The reader can understand why Denscher needs to feel this way, but nonetheless his face-saving egotism is so small-minded, his inability to think of Milly at all so disappointing, that he seems despicable, and James's ironic treatment understandable—even though the irony is sometimes so savage that it may remind us of certain passages in Stephen Crane's *Maggie, A Girl of the Streets* or *The Red Badge of Courage.* (And James may well have learned from these books, given his admiration of and friendship with the recently deceased young American writer and neighbor.)

This sequence in book 6, however, is quite different, and therefore more typical of James's treatment of Denscher's involvement with Milly throughout the novel. Here, soon after the young man finds he cannot judge his fiancée's "design," he jumps from the feeling that Milly likes him to the conclusion that, if he leaves too quickly, "what Denscher therefore would have struck at would be the root, in her soul, of a pure pleasure" (228). And later, he senses that "What Milly 'liked' was to do, it thus appeared, as she was doing: our young man's glimpse of which was just what would have been for him not less a glimpse of the peculiar brutality of shaking her off" (230). Both impressions are suspiciously helpful to Denscher, and phrases like "pure pleasure" and "peculiar brutality" sound hyperbolic. On the other hand, the narrator's use of "Denscher" in the first example (rather than "he") and "our young man's" in the second (rather than "his") suggests that the author may support these conclusions. In essence, Denscher is probably right, despite his less than pure motivation.

The pressure on Denscher becomes intense, however, when he resists the temptation to reply to Milly's "I'd do anything for Kate" (232)

with his own "Oh I know what one would do for Kate!" (232–33);
Denscher thinks, "she might for the moment have effectively laid a
trap for whatever remains of the ideal straightness in him were still
able to pull themselves together and operate" (232). Then, after he
says, "I don't feel as if I know her [Kate]—really to call know," and
after he convinces himself "that his own [remark] contained after all
no element of falsity," he feels strongly that he has arrived "at a corner—and fairly put there by his last speech; so that it depended on
him whether or no to turn it" (233).

At this moment, Milly's carriage arrives and she invites him to drive
it, assuming a "happy response" to her invitation. As Denscher's anguished ruminations suggest, he knows that his next move is crucial.
In some ways, Denscher's situation resembles that of Hurstwood in
front of the safe in *Sister Carrie*. Like Hurstwood, James's character does
not know what to do because of pressures shoving him in opposed
directions; and, as with Hurstwood, Denscher's potential action is extremely important, although it is much less easy than in Theodore
Dreiser's novel for a first-time reader of *The Wings of the Dove* to intellectualize why this is so, even though he or she will feel that it must
be the case. Dreiser lectures us about Hurstwood's perfectly understandable reasons for not comprehending the "true ethics" of the situation, the point being that we must not condemn this inability. Then,
the novelist uses chance to solve the dilemma: the safe slams shut.

James does not lecture us about anything and allows Denscher to
shut his own safe when he blurts out, "Oh yes, I'll go with you with
pleasure. It's a charming idea" (234). Denscher subsequently puzzles
out that the reason for his words is his "wish, in civil acknowledge-
ment, to oblige *her*" (235); he then goes on to soothing speculations
about the winsome ways of American "spontaneity." Because we have
been part of Denscher's consciousness, we may find his conclusion too
pat, too simple. But James is no help to us here. Although he implies
that Denscher's decision derives somehow from his character, this is as
far as the author will go. Denscher "presently became conscious of
having decided" and later thinks, "*If he had been drifting* it settled itself
in the manner of a bump" (my italics). The equivocation is not merely
Denscher's; it is also James's. Both character and creator are uncertain.

While Milly is dressing, Denscher tries to keep at bay "the sense of
having rounded his corner. He had so rounded it that he felt himself
lose even the option of taking advantage of Milly's absence to retrace
his steps." The young man who before had been casual about time now

realizes that "If he might have turned tail, vulgarly speaking, five min-
utes before, he couldn't turn tail now; he must simply wait there with
his consciousness charged to the brim" (235). Although the metaphor
of "rounding a corner" is expressed actively, and thus suggests Denscher's responsibility, the reader is sufficiently aware of the pressures on
the young man that his "action" here seems to be of a peculiarly passive
kind. Moreover, in the original version of the text, James expressed
the idea passively: "his corner was turned" (430). The question of responsibility is not clear; nor, one is led to believe, is it ever really clear
in situations as complex as this.

Kate now arrives to visit Milly, and Denscher does what he does so
frequently when his conscience has been bruised: he shoves responsibility toward someone else: "It's not I who am responsible for her, my
dear. It seems to me it's you" (236). There is truth in this statement,
but not all the truth, and Denscher's attempt to foist blame on his
fiancée is demeaning. We understand why he speaks this way; nonetheless, he disappoints us. Kate's easy support of Denscher's success
with Milly is another cause of frustration for him: here and throughout
the novel he cannot really understand why she is so comfortable about
his machinations and, tortured by insecurity, he suspects that she does
not love him. Therefore, he demands that she "swear" that "You do
'like me.' Since it's all for that, you know, that I'm letting you do—
well, God knows what with me."

Because the clear implication of this demand is that, if Kate does
not capitulate, he will "chuck" Milly, she calls his bluff and challenges
him to do so. The result of the somewhat comic interchange that follows—he vacillates between a "vision of escape" and a desire for palpable affection from Kate while she rubs his nose in her image of his
weakness—is that she achieves "one of her usual victories": He says,
"I'll do all you wish" (238). Again, it is almost impossible to decide
what would be a fair response to either character. Denscher seems at
once an equivocating ass and a person tortured by just and understandable doubts;[6] Kate seems at once a shrew (and we have been told earlier
about her frustration with masculine weakness) and a picturesque, impressive woman in response to whom a "man of any taste" would want
to show "imagination, tact, positively even humour" (238).

The encounter culminates with Denscher's decision to pursue his
relation with Milly, but again it is impossible to explain why this has
happened. Clearly the qualities of persons have been involved, but so
too have the dynamics of their relation as it has developed in a partic-

ular place over time. The occasion ends with Denscher's sense of having "so rounded his corner that it wasn't a question of a word more or less" (239). (This repetition of the expression too was expressed passively in the original text: "His corner was so turned . . . less" [430].) If asked to explain how this has happened or to evaluate it from an ethical perspective, we would be wise to shrug our shoulders, point to the text, and encourage the questioner to peruse it with attention.

The Ordeal of Merton Denscher and the Beatification of Milly Theale

A second resonant "occasion" worthy of analysis spreads itself out over chapters 4 and 5 of book 10. Viewed primarily through Denscher's consciousness, the occasion begins on Christmas Day as the young man—tormented by worries about Lord Mark and filled with wonder at a letter he has received from the dying Milly—searches for Kate at the squalid home of her sister, Mrs. Condrip; the sequence is climaxed by Kate throwing Milly's unopened letter into the fire. Discussion of this sequence, unlike the analysis of book 6, chapter 5, will focus less on specific details, more on the way in which certain aspects of the two chapters are related to the rest of the novel.

One obvious function of the chapters is to remind the reader of the humiliation Kate feels about her family's failure and her disgust with her sister's environment. A second related purpose is to illuminate the destructive differences between the personalities of the two lovers and their ways of viewing the world. These differences, originally important as causes of Kate and Denscher's attraction, are now, because of the couple's involvement with Milly, crucial as motives for estrangement and, in the novel's last scene, separation. The first function of the sequence need not be belabored: in book 1 we learned of Kate's hatred for an atmosphere of failure; here, Denscher's perception informs us of how horribly inappropriate an environment of ugliness is to Kate. We are also invited to ponder the possible importance of her drive to escape this trap and the ways in which this motive should diminish our desire to condemn her actions.

The second function requires a lengthier discussion. Crucial to Denscher's selfhood is a need to reconcile his actions with a confused but potent sense of those "traditional" values—honor, for example—probably derived from his education and family (we learn early that his dead father was a minister). This yearned-for unity of concept and action is seemingly what "straightness" means to the young man. Although Kate is not contemptuous of her fiancé's desire to be "straight"—in fact, this probably helps attract her in the first place, given her father's lack of "straightness"—her admiration for traditional values is much less strong than his. Her essential needs are more basic, more primitive than his: a "narrow family feeling," as she says at one point, and a drive to escape squalor and complete herself by being surrounded with and expressed through beautiful things.

By the time we arrive at this occasion in book 10, the differences between Kate and Denscher are almost impossible to mend, despite their continuing sexual attraction and the way in which each person has become important to the selfhood of the other. The tension is particularly acute in Denscher, because, in cultivating his relation with Milly, he has had, as Kate discerns, "to take yourself in hand. You've had to do yourself violence" (393). His most terrifying fear is that, in Venice, when he does not tell Milly he is engaged, he not only may have destroyed the chance to prolong her life, but he also may have misinterpreted his feeling for Kate: Kate tells him that he is in love with Milly, and Denscher knows that Kate may be right. Intensifying his fear and self-doubt is his suspicion that, by refusing in Venice to "give Kate away," he may have defended a woman who has told Lord Mark about her engagement—and not out of a need to reveal the truth but so he will inform Milly and hasten her death. A complicating fear—unacknowledged by Denscher but nonetheless present—is that Kate may not love him and may now favor Lord Mark. Mark's behavior in Venice contributes to this fear, as does Denscher's early-morning discovery of the impecunious lord in Aunt Maud's carriage. These emotions coalesce at the beginning of chapter 5 when Denscher is driven to cry out, "My dear child, I'm not trying to 'fix' anything; but I'm extremely tormented and I seem not to understand. What has the brute to do with us anyway?" (387).

Kate, whose impatience and frustration with Denscher's equivocations and implied accusations are frequently in evidence during this scene, produces a plausible-sounding explanation of Lord Mark's behavior during the last few weeks. Then, during the remainder of the meeting, she refuses to discuss her father with Denscher, tells him that he now loves Milly, and deduces that when Denscher offers Milly's letter as a "tribute" to her own "sacrifice" (392) in Venice he is really trying to assuage his conscience. Finally, she "jerked the thing into the flame" (394). Kate is impossible to read throughout this sequence. Her explanations about Lord Mark sound reasonable; on the other hand, because of her aims and toughness, Denscher's fears may be justified. Moreover, given her peculiar values, Kate probably could have revealed her engagement to Lord Mark and still believed that she had been "playing fair with her [Milly]. And I did . . . play fair" (393).

The reasons for Kate's destruction of the letter also remain mysterious. The gesture may be—at last—a spontaneous, uncontrolled response from this extremely controlled person to her jealousy of Milly and her frustration with Denscher's self-deceptive maunderings. Certainly many things that her fiancé has said or insinuated have been insulting—insulting, that is, if his fears about Lord Mark are unjustified—and her action may be driven by total frustration with Denscher. On the other hand, the burning of the letter may be strategic: being convinced by now that Denscher will receive money from Milly, Kate may be performing a calculated action designed to break his unhealthy relation with the dead girl before it destroys their engagement. Again, we do not know, and clearly neither does James. The logic of the novelist's characterization and plot has driven him to create a situation where almost everything is open-ended: each reader, therefore, must interpret and judge in his own way, based upon his own values and response to the text. At the same time, each reader must recognize that any provisional meaning may immediately and easily deconstruct.

At the point in the scene when Denscher asks "What has the brute to do with us anyway?" (387), the question is not only a request for information; but also an anguished plea provoked by the young man's unconscious fear and recognition of resemblance between himself and his "double." Most readers will discern this. Most also should be aware of a certain ethical-metaphysical force in the query. As has been pointed out, Denscher is almost obsessed with a need to behave in a civilized fashion—to be "straight," or to create an "ideal straightness"; he is also increasingly more fearful that he has been a "brute"—a word (with its variations) that he occasionally applies to himself, but more frequently to Lord Mark, who becomes an unconscious scapegoat for Denscher's guilt. Several critics have observed the animal imagery in *The Wings of the Dove* and commented on the implications of the imagery, the plot, and the actions of the characters for the novel's treatment of that loose amalgam of attitudes commonly referred to as Social Darwinism. Kate at home suggests a magnificent, trapped animal, and both she and Lord Mark warn Milly about the predatory nature of good English society. This is not nature red in tooth and claw, but the drives to survive and dominate have not been eliminated in the sophisticated world.

The ramifications of Denscher's question are large, therefore, and although the precise answer to it is impossible to state, what James implies is, "a great deal." People do prey upon one another—perhaps a metaphorical cannibalism may be the basis of human relations—an idea that James has played with most obviously in *The Sacred Fount.* James does not merely satirize, however, the almost trite paradox that civilized codes may organize or disguise the brutal; nor does he lament, as the narrator writes in *The Spoils of Poynton,* the "high brutality of good intentions." A component of Kate and Denscher's relation is sexual attraction and edgy competitiveness, a galvanic feeling the disappearance of which by the end of the novel makes their encounters "bland," "superficial" and, as Denscher would have said "had he so far faced it as to describe it— . . . so damned civil" (397).

Moreover, a major source of Kate's attractiveness is that combination of health, vigor, and energy which might be called "animal" (and which Denscher calls "talent for life" [397]). Another source is her impulse to dominate her environment: she is not content like her sister to whine about her sad lot and allow herself to be pushed under by males or circumstances. She can adopt disguises, invent strategies, persevere—she can adapt—and by the end she is well on her way to transcending the genteel poverty her family's selfish, ineffectual, or unlucky males have created. As Ruth Yeazell observes, Kate has qualities of the artist, ones undoubtedly significant in preserving her attractiveness despite actions that might legitimately be called immoral. We should also discern the qualities of a magnificent healthy animal, filled with a life force that will not be snapped or weakly sublimated. Kate at times may remind readers capable of entertaining grotesque comparisons of Buck in Jack London's *Call of the Wild,* a novella published around the same time as *The Wings of the Dove* and likewise concerned, as was so much fiction of the period, with the beauty and horror of a world viewed from a quasi-Darwinian perspective and with the clash between codes appropriate to this world and ones better suited to a somewhat nostalgically viewed Christian universe.

In James's novel, contrasting at least ostensibly with a value system influenced by Darwin is one influenced by Christ, because, as many critics have recognized, James wanted to remind readers of the ethics and metaphysics of Christianity. It is relatively easy to point to the

Christian allusions in the novel—in the title, for example, in Susan and Milly's scene in the Alps (where Milly looks down on the kingdoms of the earth), in the former's reference at the party in Venice to a painting by Veronese, in Milly's white dress, in her seemingly generous Christmas response to treachery, in the resemblance between Denscher's change of heart and a conversion experience, and so on.[7] It is difficult to explain satisfactorily the function of these allusions, however, and it is impossible to determine James's attitude toward them. What is peculiar about some is that they seem almost frivolous or parodic, as if James were daring us (and perhaps himself) to take them seriously. The biblical resonance of the name Lord Mark (who becomes Milly's "way") is a case in point. Another obvious example is that the mythologizing of Milly takes place in somewhat sentimental tête-a-têtes between Denscher and Aunt Maud, in which Milly is called "stupendous" and Maud "enjoyed the perfection of the pathos" (368).

Milly may metamorphose into a type of Christ because of Denscher's immense need to feel cleansed and shriven. At the end, his consciousness is terribly divided, and in pondering a relation with someone he imagines to be pure, he may be trying, unconsciously, to create a therapeutic supreme fiction. Milly may, at the end, be purposely playing a Christ-like role—or more accurately, assuming a Christ-like identity, the last one of a series (an example of which is "American girl") that she has been trying on, since her arrival in Europe, in her passionate attempt to create a self before succumbing to illness. Certainly one difference between Milly at the beginning of her adventure and at the end is that she finally recognizes her value. Despite her vast wealth and the effusions of her friend Susan Stringham, Milly is not aware of her worth—either materially or existentially, the latter somehow linked to her money—when she comes to Europe.

Although she is skeptical about the lionizing she experiences in England (climaxed by her epiphany at the country house, Matcham), her treatment there is instructive, and after arriving in Venice she is willing to use her wealth almost unscrupulously through the Mafia-like Eugenio "as a counter-move to fate" (263). Initially, she wishes only isolation, even from "Susie who would have drowned her very self for her" (263). Perhaps then, stimulated by several factors—her brooding about wealth, her response to the image of the dove earlier thrust upon her, her constantly revealed desire to shield herself from pity, her wish to see and provoke the best in people—perhaps, driven by these and other motives, Milly decides to become consciously Christ-like: she will love, bestow gifts, and, in death, generously forgive others their trespasses.

James's use of Christian references, his treatment of Denscher, and his unwillingness to deal with Milly's dying directly may tease readers into speculations about lurking metaphysical meaning. James's methods have also led some readers into sentimentalizing or oversimplifying the character of the "dove." At this point, the discussion of the novel will move far away from the occasion in book 10 with which this section began. But before this chapter on *The Wings of the Dove* is concluded, it should be stressed that James's treatment of Milly is rich and complicated. Since the tendency of critics who are unimpressed with Milly is to see in her a soft, fuzzy, unbelievable icon of Christ, it is important to observe her shrewd, edgy capacity for smelling out the "machinations of sympathy" (166) and dealing with them. At times she copes with the emotion's potentially demeaning effects by a rueful, reluctant, and attractive acceptance. Upon meeting Denscher in the British Museum, for example, she observes, "he was now acting from a particular desire, determined either by new facts or new fantasies, to be like every one else, simplifyingly kind to her. He had caught on already as to manner. . . . The defect of it in general—if she might so ungraciously criticise—was that, by its sweet universality, it made relations rather prosaically a matter of course" (181).

Milly, then, is very sensitive to the inauthentic or unhealthy motives influencing others in their relations with her. At the same time, however, because of her illness and her conviction that she is dying, she must accept what people will give, despite the dubious quality of the gifts (she has had enough of European nature when she leaves the Alps, and she decides in the British Museum that she lacks the time to benefit from the "Turners and Titians"). Her problem throughout, therefore, is sorting out the potentially useful from the potentially deleterious. At her first London dinner party, for example, Lord Mark's cynical comments "alarm" her (104); yet she chooses to immerse herself in his world since "It was queerly a question of the short run and the consciousness proportionately crowded" (105). Later, just prior to the key scene at Matcham, Milly accepts the "protective mantle, a shelter with the weight of an Eastern carpet" from Aunt Maud, even though she knows that "An Eastern carpet, for wishing-purposes of one's own, was a thing to be on rather than under" (134).

Then, at Matcham, as Milly and Lord Mark move slowly toward the Bronzino painting, she is disturbed—she senses a violation—by the "kind eyes" that fondle her as she walks her "gauntlet." At the same time, she thinks that something positive, even if ineffable, may come of the experience, so she abandons herself to it: "Once more things melted together—the beauty and the history and the facility and the splendid mid-summer glow: it was a sort of magnificent maximum, the pink dawn of an apotheosis coming so curiously soon" (137).[8] Later, Milly realizes that one reason for immersing herself in these moments is "that she had in a manner plunged into it to escape from something else" (140). Throughout, she chooses to interpret and respond to certain events and characters in ways that bring maximum benefit for her, given her possible demise and the options available to postpone it. What is being argued here about Milly is that, like Kate and Denscher—like most humans, James implies—she has a well-developed ability to rationalize; this capability keeps her alive until Lord Mark's words cause her to turn "her face to the wall."

The relevance of Milly's qualities to the Christian implications of the novel is worth discussing briefly. If one regards the capacity to feel pity as a Christian virtue, for example, one may also recognize James's Blakean, Emersonian, even Nietzschean, distrust of it. Pity, James suggests, may be a disguised form of selfishness—a means of providing oneself with a warm emotional bath; pity may also weaken the object of one's concern. Milly cannot afford to be pitied because she may then feel sorry for herself, and she must preserve a certain psychic toughness if she hopes to survive. She finally may have been destroyed by the sudden debilitating effect of self-pity when she discovers she has been deceived, even though afterwards she is able to recover a temporary equilibrium.

If we interpret Milly's ostensible generosity to Denscher as a Christian act, we may discern implications not unequivocally positive, although the gesture combines the elements of the moral and the aesthetic, the disinterested and the picturesque, into a blend James usually finds admirable. The problem is that there is something almost perverse in Denscher's cherishing of his memory of the letter he could not open—this icon he has been unable to preserve. In addition, in the subtext of the last encounter between the two lovers, there is a hint of the sanctimonious and priggish in Denscher's desire to "test" Kate by seeing what she will do with the letters from Milly's solicitors. Here, Denscher suggests the zealot who cannot live in the world or relate in a healthy way to other people. In sum, if one were to judge from the results of Milly's action, one might conclude that they are not unambiguous. Milly's consistent desire has been for other people to act well; yet here, at the end, we cannot be certain about Denscher's present or future behavior. The wings of this particular dove, in fact, may eventually suffocate Denscher, rather than liberating him to fly alone. And all the reader can conclude about the effect of Milly's ostensible beneficence on the relation between Kate and Denscher is epitomized in the defiant resignation of Kate's final words: "We shall never be again as we were!" (403).

Chapter Eight

The Golden Bowl: The Greatness of the Good Heroine

Background

Genesis and text.   James completed reading proofs of *The Wings of the Dove* in the summer of 1902. Concurrently, he worked on several short stories, most notably "The Beast in the Jungle" and "The Birth-place," at least two of which he needed to flesh out *The Better Sort,* the volume of short fiction published in 1903. During the winter in London James wrote the biography of the amateur sculptor William Wetmore Story, the notes for which he had made several years before. Although James did not enjoy the project, Houghton, Mifflin was so pleased with *William Wetmore Story and His Friends* that James was invited to prepare a biography of his friend, the recently deceased American poet-diplomat James Russell Lowell. James refused this offer, not wishing to involve himself again with the life of someone about whom, he felt, there was little to say. During the winter of 1903 James also read proofs for *The Ambassadors,* which at long last had begun to be serialized. A final significant project, about which more will be said later, was his series of articles about French writers—Balzac, Flaubert, and Zola.

James began *The Golden Bowl* in late May, had written over 100,000 words by late October, and had commenced extensive revision by November. Although he remarked in a 8 January 1904 letter to Howells that he had finished the novel, he did not mail its last sections to his agent, James Pinker, until 21 July. On 24 August he sailed for the United States, a trip he had been planning since November 1903. James was apprehensive about his visit but had high hopes for the benefits to be derived from it: a few well-paid lectures; serialization of his "impressions" and later book publication; perhaps material for a new novel; perhaps also a contract with Scribner's for a monumental, definitive edition of his works.

In the United States, Charles Scribner's Sons published 2,000 copies of an attractive two-volume edition of *The Golden Bowl* on 10 November 1904; in England, Methuen published 3,000 copies of a one-volume edition of the same text on 10 February 1905.[1] The revised and definitive two-volume New York Edition was published by Scribner's in 1909. The differences between this final version of *The Golden Bowl* and the two earlier editions are not large but nonetheless worthy of note: preceding the text is James's preface; two photographs of London locations suggestive of the "golden bowl" shop and of Portland Place act as frontispieces to each volume; the six "parts" of the earlier texts become six "books," with chapters numbered consecutively within each "book" rather than throughout the novel; the occasional word has been changed; and many commas have been excised.

Source and influence. James first referred to the idea upon which *The Golden Bowl* is based in a 28 November 1892 *Notebooks* entry made during a period in which he was devoting himself to plays and short fiction. By the time he completed the entry, several ingredients that appear in the later novel were already present—the extremely close relation of the American father and daughter, for example, and the romantic entanglement of their spouses. At this point, however, James's intention was to create only a "little tale" about "the pathetic simplicity and good faith of the father and daughter in their abandonment."[2] Significantly, no reference was made to what the American girl would do when she began to feel abandoned, except to console and seek consolation from her equally bereft and powerless father.

After his *Guy Domville* humiliation, James returned briefly to the idea on 14 February 1895, as he tried to cheer himself up and gain inspiration to write a short international novel for Henry Harper. Although James was eager to churn out between 60,000 and 75,000 words for Harper, he was worried about his ability to handle "the adulterine element in the subject."[3] Perhaps for this reason he did not plunge immediately into it. Undoubtedly important also was that, in trying to honor a commitment to the *Atlantic Monthly* for three short tales, James wrote one novella—*The Spoils of Poynton*—which led to his several-year immersion in an English milieu, not an international one. Even during this period, however, a few brief *Notebooks* entries suggest his continuing interest in the idea about "the Father and Daughter, with the husband of the one and the wife of the other entangled in a mutual passion, an intrigue."[4]

Uncharacteristically, the preface to the novel is silent about its source, a fact that has probably helped to encourage scholarly sleuthing. For some scholars *The Golden Bowl* is a novel grounded deeply in James's direct experience—his speculations, for example, about the childhood triangle of his father and mother and an aunt who lived in their household; or James's very recent infatuation with Jocelyn Persse, the young man whom he had met at a wedding just after beginning *The Golden Bowl*.[5] Scholars also suggest a work rooted even more deeply in the author's literary experience. Reasonable cases have been made, for example, for the influence of such diverse writers as Shakespeare, Keats, Coleridge, Eliot, Balzac, Hawthorne, Poe, Browning, Paul Bourget, Ibsen, and William and Henry James, Sr.[6] Plausible cases have also been made for the influence of a large selection of James's own fiction—from an early short story about an Italian nobleman entitled "The Last of the Valerii," to his many experiments in handling risqué material, and to the very recent "The Beast in the Jungle." Certainly the confidence with which James began his novel (evinced by his willingness to commit himself at that time to an American trip after the completion of *The Golden Bowl*), the ostensible ease with which he wrote it, and his satisfaction when he finished the novel suggest a subject and a treatment thoroughly assimilated and understood.

A crucial influence on the novel was James's introduction during Christmas 1902 to a real golden bowl given by George I to the Lamb House owner's child, whose christening the monarch had attended. According to Leon Edel, James studied the bowl and asked many questions about it. Clearly he was fascinated by this royal commemorative gift, intimately related to the talismanic ceremonies of marriage and christening, yet resonant also of a passage in Ecclesiastes suggesting mortality and evanescent perfection: remember the Lord, says the preacher, before "ever the silver cord be loosed, or the golden bowl be broken, or the pitcher be broken at the fountain."[7]

Extremely important also, particularly as a source for James's treatment of Maggie Verver in the novel's second volume are several attitudes most clearly revealed in two places—in a series of critical discussions about Balzac, Flaubert, Zola, and the Italian romantic writer Gabriele D'Annunzio; and in a little-known 1902 tale called

"The Story in It." Evident in James's commentary on the great French novelists is his admiration for their willingness to dedicate themselves totally and confidently to their fictional goals. James is impressed by their uncompromising fidelity to and portrayal of what the story's male protagonist, Colonel Voyt, calls "their sense of life. . . . They do what they feel, and they feel more things than we." When Voyt contrasts the French fiction to the "novel of British and American manufacture," in which the "sense of life [is] the sense of puppies and kittens," he asks, "When it comes to any account of a relation, say, between a man and a woman—I mean an intimate or a curious or a suggestive one— where are we compared to them?"[8]

Evident also in James's remarks about the French writers is his admiration for Flaubert's obsession with form and—as opposed to Flaubert's ironic distancing from his characters—Balzac's "coercion of total intensity," his "hunger on the part of his nature to take in all freedom another nature—take it by a direct process of the senses" (211).[9] In contemplating their careers, James observes three men eager to risk almost everything so that each may communicate his own special "sense of life" in his own idiosyncratic manner. James's desire to emulate the French novelists undoubtedly influenced much of the fiction written during this period. Arguably, however, the desire is a particularly important source for this novel: for his decision to lavish all of his peculiar, self-reflexive, and highly developed technical skill—the almost claustrophobic handling of point of view, for example, the alternatingly abstract and operatic style, the implausibly tight, symmetrical plot and balancing of characters, the proliferation of parallel scenes, the daring use of minor characters—on a subject which James knew in advance would be to some readers scabrous, to many others much ado about nothing.

In addition, exemplified in "The Story in It" and in James's essays on the continental writers—most clearly in the discussions of Flaubert and D'Annunzio—is an uneasiness about a weakness least important in Balzac but nonetheless present in each writer. In his essay on D'Annunzio, James complains that "sexual passion . . . insists on remaining for him only the act of a moment, beginning and ending in itself and disowning any representative character. . . . Shut out from the rest of life, shut out from all fruition and assimilation, it has no more dignity than—to use a homely image—the boots and shoes that we see, in the corridors of promiscuous hotels, standing, often in double pairs, at the doors of rooms" (295).

In "The Story in It," a Mrs. Blessingbourne laments the lack, in the French fiction which she devours, of a "decent woman"—of a woman in whom passion and unhappiness can lead to behavior both good and "interesting" (317–18). Colonel Voyt maintains the impossibility of making "the adventures of innocence" interesting; he asks rhetorically, "What is a situation undeveloped but a subject lost? If a relation stops, where's the story? If it doesn't stop, where's the innocence?" He concludes, "It seems to me you must choose" (320). On the final page of the D'Annunzio essay, composed while he was writing *The Golden Bowl,* James asks: "Need the aesthetic adventure [by which he means the portrayal of sexual relations], in a word, organized for real discovery, give us no more comforting news of success? Are there not, so to speak, finer possible combinations? are there not safeguards against futility that in the example before us were but too presumably absent?" (295–96). What is suggested by such passages is that a crucial influence on *The Golden Bowl* was not only James's desire to emulate these European writers but to improve on them by creating, in Maggie Verver, a heroine who was "really furnished," "finely civilized"— in other words, a character who was passionate, virtuous, and interesting.[10]

Another probable major influence on James's novel was his desire, in his handling of goodness and sexual relations, to achieve something that he himself had not achieved to his own satisfaction. As many critics have observed, James was successful in portraying attractive, sensual, somewhat amoral women. Charlotte Stant is only one in a long tradition of such types, and, in a very real sense, the best source of this character is much of James's earlier fiction. To a certain extent Maggie Verver also belongs to two interrelated Jamesian traditions—free spirit and American girl—the most recent significant example of the latter being Milly Theale in *The Wings of the Dove.* Yet although Milly, Nanda Brookenham, Maisie Farange, Fleda Vetch, and Isabel Archer possess virtuous qualities, none is shown to be unequivocally capable of the passion rooted in sex that Maggie comes to possess. It seems probable, therefore, that a crucial source of this dimension of *The Golden Bowl* is James's intention to compete against himself and continue to grow as an artist—like the esteemed writer (undoubtedly Shakespeare) of "The Birthplace," like the much venerated Balzac (whose capacity for further growth had been cut short by death at fifty), and unlike Flaubert and Zola who, despite their achievements had, according to James, continued to write after losing their talents.

The Follies of Goodness

Early in *The Golden Bowl*, as Prince Amerigo wanders restlessly in London just after his marriage arrangements have been completed, he remembers a conversation with his fiancée, Maggie Verver, about her incredibly rich widower father. Amerigo had remarked that Adam Verver is a *"real* galantuomo. . . . He seems to me simply the best man I've ever seen in my life." Amerigo's compliment leads to a consideration of the source of Adam's admirable character (and, as Donald Mull suggests, his wealth) which to the young Italian is mysterious because of Adam's lack of an obvious style. Maggie is not surprised by her father's effect because "It's his goodness that has brought him out." But Amerigo disagrees: "Ah darling, goodness, I think, never brought any one out. Goodness, when it's real, precisely, rather keeps people in." (1:6–7).

The conversation suggests that the amiable differences between the two attractive young people derive to a certain extent—as is so often the case in James's international fiction—from their national backgrounds. It is suggested further that the quality of "goodness" is related somehow to what Amerigo thinks of as "innocence," "imagination," "the American good faith," and, most essentially, "the romantic disposition." Amerigo remarks that "You Americans are almost incredibly romantic," and Maggie agrees: "Of course we are. That's just what makes everything so nice for us." At this point Amerigo chides her gently: "You see too much—that's what may sometimes make you difficulties. When you don't, at least, . . . see too little." Yet despite his awareness of the "follies of the romantic disposition," he thinks, a bit grudgingly, that "there seemed somehow no follies in theirs—nothing, one was obliged to recognize, but innocent pleasures, pleasures without penalties" (1:10–11).

A few days later and almost immediately prior to the wedding, Charlotte Stant, Maggie's old school friend and the Prince's former lover, entices the somewhat apprehensive Amerigo into joining her in an ostensible search for Maggie's wedding present. During their walk Charlotte reveals that her real purpose is to "be as we are now and as we used to be, for one small hour—or say for two" (1:96). As they talk, the topic of goodness is again alluded to, this time as exemplified by Maggie. Charlotte remarks, "She's not selfish enough. . . . There's nothing, absolutely, that one *need* do for her. . . . if she loves you. She lets it go." Then, she becomes almost obviously insulting about her supposed friend: "She lets everything go but her own disposition to be kind to you. It's of herself that she asks efforts—so far as she ever *has* to ask them. She hasn't, much. She does everything herself. And that's terrible." The Prince seems surprised by the vehemence that Charlotte's by now only barely disguised resentment and condescension have forced into her words. He repeats "with propriety": "Terrible?" (1:101–2).

Thus encouraged, Charlotte develops her theme, first somewhat impersonally, then becoming personal and drawing her moral: "such people as you and I are not. . . . Well, not good enough not rather to feel the strain. We happen each, I think, to be of the kind that are easily spoiled." Amerigo now seems to recognize his former mistress's innuendo, so, refusing to accept her use of the personal pronoun, he pushes her back a little: "May not one's affection for her do something more for one's decency, as you call it, than her own generosity—her own affection, *her* 'decency'—has the unfortunate virtue to undo?" (1:102).

But despite Amerigo's attempts to keep Charlotte at safe distance, some remarks have interested him; he therefore returns to an earlier observation: "What it comes to—one can see what you mean—is the way she believes in one." Then he adds strangely, "That is if she believes at all." Finally, he asks, "And why . . . should it be terrible?" Charlotte now thrusts: "Because it's always so—the idea of having to pity people"; but Amerigo finds her implication unattractive and parries: "Not when there's also with it the idea of helping them." Charlotte tries again, more gently this time: "Yes, but if we can't help them?" But again Amerigo rejects the implied offer, although he accepts Charlotte's use of the personal pronoun: "We *can*—we always can. That is, . . . if we care for them. And that's what we're talking about." The Mephistophelean Charlotte, discerning the graceful rebuke, admits defeat and, as the scene ends, says, "It's just what I meant" (1:103).

Many readers sympathize with Charlotte and find her panache— Maggie calls it "greatness" (1:180)—extremely attractive.[11] Occasions such as the above, however, suggest the danger of sentimentalizing her: from the moment of her arrival she encourages the Prince to take sexual advantage of Maggie's goodness, while also revealing her reservations about this virtue. Maggie, Charlotte implies, is foolishly, unintelligently good. Her virtue is too easy; Maggie should be pitied for trusting so completely. Because Charlotte's attitudes are so obviously self-serving, they reflect at this point more on her frustration and resentment than on the limitations of Maggie's character. Yet, given the background of Charlotte and Amerigo, the reader must fear for the future of someone for whom most things in life are "nice" or "beautiful."

Moreover, we may wonder why the Prince finds so interesting Charlotte's implied criticisms of Maggie. Perhaps he is merely being polite. Perhaps because of his former relation with Charlotte and her sexual allure he is, in a guarded, decorous way, keeping his options open. But perhaps he responds to something in Maggie's personality that not only puzzles him, but already—even before marriage and despite his attraction to her—irritates him somewhat. Intimated by the Prince's "That's if she believes at all," for example, is a slight uneasiness: is there, he may wonder, in Maggie's propensity to be pleased by everything an inability to care passionately about anything? Can Maggie assign values, can she discriminate? In particular, does she really know what I am worth (as one invents these questions, one also thinks of Browning's "My Last Dutchess")? This early, one's guesses about the possible source of Amerigo's slight uneasiness must be very tentative. But Charlotte's meaning is clear: in Maggie's eagerness to trust totally there is an almost willfully obtuse attitude toward human nature. The negative suggestions about the Ververs' goodness are only in the novel's subtext. James's scrutiny of the virtue, however—his examination of whether it "keeps people in" or "brings them out"—becomes more obvious as the plot develops.

Later, after the birth of the Principino, after Adam and Charlotte's marriage, and after Maggie and Adam have, for several months, devoted many hours to each other while encouraging their spouses to attend social engagements, Charlotte, at a magnificent party, says to Fanny Assingham, "I've simply to see the truth of the matter—see that Maggie thinks more on the whole of fathers than of husbands." After Fanny tries to defend Maggie by asserting that she "adores" Amerigo, Charlotte replies, as if to a noncomprehending child, "I don't say she doesn't adore him. What I say is that she doesn't think of him. One of those conditions doesn't always at all stages involve the other. This is just *how* she adores him." When Fanny splutters, "You ought to be absolutely happy. You live with such *good* people," Charlotte responds angrily, "Does one ever put into words anything so fatuously rash? It's a thing that must be said, in prudence, *for* one—by somebody who's so good as to take the responsibility: the more it gives one always a chance to show one's best manners by not contradicting it" (1:257–58).

Because by now it has been implied strongly that Charlotte's marriage is terminally boring, the reader knows she is biased. Charlotte's words, however, may suggest several possibilities: that there is, for example, in Maggie's adoration a mindless, aggravating inattention; that the Ververs' goodness may be so bland, conventional, and unobservant as to deserve condemnation, not praise. Charlotte earlier mentions their "make-believe renewals of their old life. They were fairly at times, the dear things, like children playing at paying visits." She also describes Maggie's anxiety about Adam's possible illness and says, "She worries easily, you know." Moreover, "If he had been too ill I wouldn't have left him" (1:252–53). What galls her is that Maggie's solicitude is not only childish but insulting. Charlotte's barely suppressed anger may be unfair; it also may have some justification.

Later, there are further hints of Maggie's unconscious presumptuousness: the party hosted by the Ververs, for example, in which, "so far as it referred itself with any confidence of emphasis to a hostess, seemed to refer itself preferentially, well-meaningly, and perversely, to Maggie" (1:321). And in the earlier crucial scene climaxed by the passionate kiss between the Prince and Charlotte, the latter tracks down Amerigo in a grubby cab because her carriage has been taken by Maggie, who runs an errand for Adam.

There is a considerable amount of irony in James's treatment of the buildup to the kiss between the two lovers, because in the references to the "conscious care" which they say they are taking for their spouses, in their use of words such as "wonderful," "beautiful," and "sacred," they show that they are rationalizing a powerful sexual attraction.[12] There is also irony in James's treatment of the scene at Matcham where they consummate their relation. Here, in this Easter encounter as they search for the cathedral at Gloucester, the god they worship is not Christian; he is Eros. Ironic also in the many specific references to time in the chapter and in Charlotte's "we must employ our time" (1:362) are the echoes of Marvell's poem: Amerigo's mistress is anything but coy.

On the other hand, it is difficult not to sympathize with the lovers. Volume 1 is primarily the Prince's, and because we experience his response to events we feel his extreme frustration, boredom, even humiliation as when, for example, he says "very vehemently" about Maggie and Adam, "How can I not feel more than anything else how they adore together my boy?" (1:307). Through a variety of means it is suggested in the latter part of the volume that the Ververs' innocence, virtue—in other words their goodness—has become to a certain extent complacent, smug, discriminating only to themselves, and ultimately, selfish. Their goodness, moreover, is essentially passive: they do in their marriages what has always come easily and naturally. Contrasted to this somewhat flabby goodness, Charlotte's activity may seem attractive, particularly when, at Matcham, she exclaims to her once and future lover, "I risk the cracks" (1:359), as they reminisce about the gilt bowl in Bloomsbury they had chosen not to buy.

Much of the narrative interest in volume 1 derives from James's suspenseful buildup to the moments of infidelity: we sense early that there may be problems in Maggie's marriage, we have been shown that Adam's marriage is primarily of convenience, we have been led to see how the goodness of Maggie and Adam has been combining with the attraction between the Prince and Charlotte to create sexual excitement, and we have been rewarded with a marvelously sensual scene at Matcham. In effect, James has written a French novel in the first volume of *The Golden Bowl*—the kind of book that the virtuous heroine in "The Story in It" immerses herself in. James's French novel is more subtle and complex than the norm; yet a major source of reader interest, of titillation, is similar.

Volume 2 is very different, however, a possibility prefigured in the lengthy "occasion" between Colonel and Fanny Assingham which closes the first volume.[13] Fanny suspects Charlotte and the Prince of infidelity and, since she has helped arrange the marriages, fears the results of their demise. While trying to cheer herself up during the midnight colloquy with her exasperating, commonsensical husband, she also prefigures the Fortunate Fall structure as well as the plot of volume 2 to an unusual degree. Maggie, Fanny predicts, will "take it all herself"; "she'll triumph"; "Her sense will have to open. . . . To what's called Evil—with a very big E"; "I like the idea of Maggie audacious and impudent—learning to be so to gloss things over. She could—she even will, yet, I believe—learn it for that sacred purpose, consummately, diabolically" (1:380–97). Particularly daring about this very long occasion is that in it James seems to think through the second volume of the novel in full view of his readers, as if he has decided to use the last chapter of volume 1 as his notebook or a scenario.

The Discovery of the Bowl

Near the end of that chapter the befuddled but now entranced Colonel Bob concludes, "Then she's a little heroine" (1:397). And of course she is. Volume 2 is very much Maggie's volume, both because her point of view dominates (much more consistently than does the Prince's in volume 1), and because her actions—no longer her passivity—propel the plot and reshape her marriage.[14] As the volume opens, the reader is plunged immediately into a stylistically dense, imagistically brilliant analysis of Maggie's "restless reverie"—spanning two chapters in the text—at the end of which "she felt very much alone," because of her "first shock of complete perception" that, despite her best efforts to share the lives of Charlotte and Amerigo, she is being "arranged apart" (2:45). Maggie's reverie is wide-ranging. She remembers, for example, surprising Amerigo by waiting at her fireside for his return from Matcham rather than at Adam's house; recognizing that "she adored and missed and desired" her husband; suspecting that she probably had "accepted too passively the funny form of our life"; deciding "to bring about a difference, touch by touch, without either of the three, and least of all her father, so much as suspecting her hand"; and discovering that she is being "treated" by Charlotte and Amerigo, who evidently do not want to share (2:3–45).

The reverie begins with an image whose meaning has been much debated by critics: that of the "outlandish pagoda" in the "blooming garden"—a figure which, for several months before the Matcham weekend, Maggie has used to explain the "arrangement . . . by which, so strikingly, she had been able to marry without breaking . . . with her past" (2:5). This image is only one of several Maggie uses to epitomize the "arrangement." At other times she thinks of "some strange, tall tower of ivory" and a "Mohametan mosque, with which no base heretic could take a liberty" (2:4). Each figure suggests the unusual beauty seemingly present in her relations with husband and father; each also suggests the peculiar, somewhat forbidding qualities of this "arrangement": Maggie recognizes how lucky her life has been; yet as time passes she finds her "high felicity" somehow disquieting and suspects that something is (or should be) wrong.

At least as important as the meaning of these images is their probable effect on the reader. We have not seen much of Maggie since early in volume 1 and, if we have been influenced by Charlotte and the Prince, we may have arrived at this point with a rather unattractive picture of the young American woman: she is innocent, unconsciously but unconscionably selfish; she is dull. Amerigo thinks of her "approximation . . . to the transmitted images of rather neutral and negative propriety that made up, in his long line, the average of wifehood and motherhood" (1:322). But the picture sketched at the beginning of volume 2 is different: Maggie is an unusually sensitive, highly imaginative, passionate woman. The taste of her consciousness is neither bland nor saccharine; it is a tantalizing blend of the sweet and the slightly acerbic.

Maggie's brief consideration of her responsibility for the possible problems in her life and her abortive attempts to share experiences with Amerigo mark the first crucial stages in her drive to redeem her marriage. Maggie's rise to heroism is not continuous; neither is she consistently nor conventionally good during her development. James throughout conveys Maggie's constant need to be "heroically improvising"; he suggests how her "part opened out and she invented from moment to moment what to say and to do" (2:33). Having in the last chapter of volume 1 allowed Fanny to draw a general outline for the novel's second half, James now seems to repeat his protagonist's question as he proceeds: given Maggie's temperament and circumstances, what would "the figure in the picture do?" (2:24). The continual surprise and excitement generated by volume 2 are in large part created by James's willingness to move inside Maggie's skin so as to answer this question.

During the almost two months between Matcham and the move to Fawns, the country estate, the most important event is Maggie's discovery of the gilt bowl; this provides certain evidence that Amerigo and Charlotte knew one another before the marriages. Prior to this discovery, Maggie, despite excruciating suspicions, lacks real knowledge. In James's equation, legitimate suspicions, plus physical proximity and ignorance, equal intense frustration. Through most of this section James applies fascinated and fascinating attention to the results of this frustration.

One result is an obsessiveness reminiscent of the tormented narrators of *The Turn of the Screw* and *The Sacred Fount*. In certain instances, such as a walk in the park with Adam, Maggie interprets every sign very subjectively. In the park scene, for example (2:84-99), she needs to feel she is competing successfully with Charlotte and that Adam shares both her suspicions and her fears about expressing them (it is impossible to judge whether Maggie's reading of Adam has any validity at this point; probably not, however). Thus, Maggie reads sinister import into Adam's seemingly innocuous, at times smugly self-satisfied statements. Another result of Maggie's frustration is a sense of powerlessness, a concomitant of which is a need to luxuriate in those moments when she herself is (or imagines herself to be) in control. At a dinner party hosted by Lord and Lady Castledean, for example, Maggie, intuiting (probably correctly) that she is being patronized, desires "to possess and use them, even to the extent of braving, of fairly defying, of directly exploiting, or possibly quite enjoying, under cover of an evil duplicity, the felt element of curiosity with which they regarded her" (2:49). Although "evil duplicity" is almost comically hyperbolic, Maggie does in a sense exploit the group: against decorum, she invites them, at the dinner itself, to a return engagement at Portland Place.

During the fortnight before the early July departure for Fawns, Maggie enjoys using Fanny "for her private benefit" and torturing her with hints that "she held her, that she made her fairly responsible for something." Despite James's willingness to put Maggie's unlovely obsessiveness on display, however, he also tries to create sympathy for her through means such as obtrusive narrative comments: he says, for example, that Maggie is "more and more magnificent now in her blameless egoism" (2:145). James wants here to do more than exonerate Maggie; he tries to make her treatment of the Assinghams seem admirable. Perhaps he wants to suggest that, for the development of Maggie's self, such consciously egotistical behavior must act as a counterweight to her earlier colorless altruism (which may really be a form of selfishness). In order to have a self, Maggie must at times indulge her needs.

A key confrontation during these days involves Fanny and Maggie; it occurs while, at her somewhat masochistic prompting, Amerigo and Charlotte again visit Matcham. At the scene's outset Maggie challenges her friend with "What awfulness, in heaven's name, is there between them? What do you believe, what do you *know*?" (2:103). As the scene proceeds the self-absorption and pain caused by her jealousy are poignantly in view. More significantly, evinced also is Maggie's ability to sublimate her pain, particularly in the oft-analyzed passage in which she reiterates her willingness to bear anything "For love" (2:117). What Maggie seems to do as she repeats this talismanic phrase is to work out, on the spot, a code of conduct; this encompasses her husband, son, father, friends, and herself—the sense that she is beginning to gain a strong, admirable, developing personality. In response to

Maggie's anguish and strength, Fanny repeatedly denies the implied accusation, in part because she fears being "dished," but primarily because she wants to relieve Maggie's distress, which she does temporarily by the end of this electric occasion.

Soon after this Maggie endures a week alone with Amerigo in London while the Ververs precede them to the summer estate. By this point, the major organizing principle helping Maggie confront her ordeal is her "fiction" about Adam: she must protect him. If she gives in to Amerigo, this "would hand her over to him bound hand and foot," something she fears because she wants "to be free, to be free to act other than abjectly for her father" (2:142).

The period is climaxed on the afternoon prior to the departure for Fawns when Maggie summons Fanny to tell her about the event occurring while she was returning from a visit to a Mr. Crichton at the British Museum. The extremely lengthy occasion is given a preliminary sense of importance when the narrator writes that Fanny felt as grave "how could she not?—as the truly pious priest might feel when confronted, behind the altar, before the festa, with his miraculous Madonna" (2:153). Maggie then speaks portentously: "Something very strange has happened, and I think you ought to know it" (2:154).

In searching for a birthday present for her father, Maggie has unearthed the "golden" bowl. Much of the first part of the occasion is viewed from Fanny's perspective, a strategy useful to James because it allows him, through a kind of disguised omniscience, to stress the significance of Maggie's behavior: the "beauty" of her decision not to condemn Fanny for meddling in the marriages, for example; the grace of Maggie's "managed quietness," her "achieved coherence"; the bravery demanded by her policy of not harming her father. An almost equally important effect—one perhaps not originally intended but nonetheless achieved as James responds to the rhythm of the scene—is the appreciation the reader gains of Fanny's own heroism, goodness, kindness, sensitivity—call it what one will—as she tries to help Maggie master her crisis.

Initially when Maggie reveals the "gilt cup" Fanny wards off Maggie's accusatory thrusts and decides that she will not be tamed by Maggie's aggressive use of the bowl.[15] Later, as Maggie begins to show the depth of her feelings about her father, her outrage that he may have been betrayed—finally her brief recognition that she herself may have been at fault "if everything really began so well?" (2:172)—Fanny discovers a key to subsequent behavior that she thinks will help both of them: Maggie's fervent need to think well of Adam. Fanny builds on this until she tells her friend to have faith in her father; then, she throws the bowl to the floor. Thus responding to an "irresistible impulse," she hopes to convince Maggie that "Whatever you meant by it—and I don't want to know *now*—has ceased to exist" (2:179).

After this amazing coup de théâtre—at once quintessentially melodramatic and forced out of the scene by the logic of the characters—there follows another remarkable coup—Amerigo's entrance—and the occasion, daringly, continues, picking up a new momentum and developing a new meaning. Several of its dimensions are worthy of note, the first being Maggie's sympathy for her husband, her wish to spare him, and her conviction that he will have "a new need of her, a need which was in fact being born between them in these very seconds" (2:186). Extraordinarily significant about this recognition is that it combines selfishness with selflessness; it is thus the type of altruistic instrumentalism that for James was the acme of ethical behavior: "It had operated within her now to the last intensity, her glimpse of the precious truth that by her helping him, helping him to help himself, as it were, she should help him to help *her*. Hadn't she fairly got into his labyrinth with him?" (2:187).

Crucial also is Amerigo's discovery that his wife is not as simple, as stupid, as he had thought. Finally, evinced again near the end is Maggie's concern for Adam—her intention to make "her care for his serenity, or at any rate for the firm outer shell of his dignity, all marvellous enamel, her paramount law" (2:202–3). The occasion ends with Maggie's challenge to her husband: if you are worried, "Find out for yourself!" (2:203), whether anyone else knows about your affair.

Readers who have disliked Maggie have sometimes pointed to actions such as this as proof of her reprehensible uses of power, her stepping beyond the bounds of the virtuous. In defense of her, perhaps all one needs to suggest is that she is aware of the danger of giving in too easily to Amerigo, she knows that she must plant a respect for herself firmly in his mind, and she surmises that only by putting him through a kind of trial that is also a tacit penance can she ever hope to create something permanent or positive in their marriage. In short, Maggie knows that she must be tough in order to repair their golden bowl.

Role-Playing

The novel enters its most important stage when the participants journey to Fawns for the summer. Now Maggie feels "not unlike some

young woman of the theatre who, engaged for a minor part in the
play . . . , should find herself suddenly promoted to leading lady"
(2:208). Significant about this simile is the implication in it that Maggie is now to a certain extent enjoying her predicament.

This feeling is intensified during the first few days at Fawns because
Maggie imagines herself "really in possession" and assumes she now
has something on Charlotte, who erroneously thinks "that I'm not in
possession of anything" (2:213–14). Another important factor contrib-
uting to this new positive frame of mind is Maggie's assumption that
she is "changed" for Amerigo. Because of her confidence Maggie's present goal is to create "happiness without a hole in it big enough for you
to poke in your finger. . . . The golden bowl—as it *was* to have
been. . . . The bowl without the crack" (2:216–17). Much of the interest here derives from James's dramatization of Maggie's seemingly
endless ability to rationalize her real lack of knowledge, and from the
author's fascination with how her imagination of atrocity has turned
temporarily into an imagination of beatitude. During this stage of be-
nign fiction-making, Maggie imagines having passed "from being
nothing for him [Amerigo] to being all" (2:228). The period's final
stage is Maggie's lingering over the possible plight of Charlotte. To
Maggie, she becomes the "haunted creature" enclosed in a "spacious
but suspended cage. . . . The cage was the deluded condition, and
Maggie, as having known delusion—rather!—understood the nature of
cages" (2:229). This almost masochistic reverie acts as a preliminary to
several remarkable occasions that punctuate the last part of the novel.

Undoubtedly the most famous occasion in *The Golden Bowl* begins
with Maggie prowling first within and then outside the smoking room
while Adam, Fanny, Amerigo, and Charlotte commune over a game of
bridge. The occasion ends with the "conscious perjury" of Maggie's
denial that she has anything to accuse Charlotte of. Much of the intensity of this marvelous scene derives from the rhythm and imagery of
the prose used to convey Maggie's tortured melodramatic consciousness
before she confronts Charlotte outside the house. One thinks, for example, of the passage in which Maggie considers revealing her knowledge: "Spacious and splendid, like a stage again awaiting a drama, it
was a scene she might people, by the press of her spring, either with
serenities and dignities and decencies, or with terrors and shames and
ruins, things as ugly as those formless fragments of her golden bowl
she was trying so hard to pick up" (2:236). In such passages James
seems to be calling attention consciously to the contrast between his
drama of goodness and the more typical melodramas that were written

and performed. Yet even while eschewing their moral simplicity, James preserves their emotional power. The effect is achieved here primarily because, although Maggie eventually decides not to act melodramatically, the possibility remains in the reader's mind because of the picturesque imagery by which it has first been conjured up.

Even before Maggie and Charlotte's night meeting we are told of Maggie's desire to play "the scapegoat of old" and to "live somehow for their benefit" (2:234–35). We also learn of Maggie's fear of confronting Charlotte, in large part because she worries this may provoke Charlotte into defending herself successfully in front of Adam. Maggie's greater fear, however, is of "dodging and ducking" (2:239); so, when Charlotte appears on the terrace, "Maggie came on with her heart in her hands" (2:242). From one point of view the results of the encounter are at least as bad as Maggie had feared: Charlotte to a large extent takes over the role of director or stage manager, first causing Maggie to pause in front of the window—not, in "righteous irony" but to see submissively a "picture of quiet harmonies"—one in which "full significance . . . could be no more after all than a matter of interpretation, differing always for a different interpreter" (2:243–44).

From another, probably more accurate point of view, however, Maggie achieves a purpose in tune with her deepest self: she allows Charlotte to cover up, and in so doing to reveal the brazen surface Maggie has always admired. Maggie is helped to abase herself purposely and thus to permit this "admirable creature" to utter most of the good lines by her belief that she and Amerigo are "together thus, . . . whereas Charlotte, though rising there radiantly before her, was really off in some darkness of space that would steep her in solitude and harass her with care" (2:250). Here James attempts again to be honest to his perception of Maggie's character. Suggested in her image is a perhaps natural but also mildly sadistic need to imagine Charlotte excluded from beatitude. James also suggests that Maggie persists in her role of scapegoat because she believes her virtue will be rewarded.

Unfortunately this exaltation does not last and, three days later, as Maggie prepares for a stroll, she wants to be again only "father and daughter with Adam" (2:255); she has, moreover, a desperate need to be cheered up after her earlier abasement. A reader must recognize these facts because they help to explain elements of the subsequent meeting with Adam that otherwise may be puzzling or disturbing— the pair's self-congratulatory remarks, for example. A reader should also observe the many signs that Adam has definitely become concerned about his daughter—that he suspects she is unhappy about her marriage. Read with this in mind, we may note the many twists during the scene as father and daughter try to discover the other's real state of mind, and also to prevent the truth from destroying them. Throughout, both Ververs skate on ice so thin they are in constant risk of drowning.

As well, read from this perspective the scene becomes poignant and unusually revelatory of an unsuspected depth of emotion in the poker-faced Adam Verver, whose portrayal has generated much puzzled, occasionally exasperated or indignant commentary.[16] The picture of Adam presented in the first volume is generally sympathetic, but also sometimes bemused and mildly satirical. Through much of volume 2 he is the person whom Maggie must see in order to organize her strategies of survival. Here, on the other hand, we glimpse another Adam as, after the fall, he tries to aid his daughter and confront the most important probable failure in his life.

Although space does not permit a full discussion of this long, beautifully structured occasion, several of its dimensions should be outlined. The first is the manner in which a strategy used by Maggie—she speaks of her "selfishness" about Amerigo to convince Adam she is happy—almost inadvertently leads her to express a passionate love for her husband; this, at the beginning of the scene, has been in abeyance: "When however you love in the most abysmal and unutterable way of all—why then you're beyond everything, and nothing can pull you down" (2:262). The second is how her "high hypocrisy" leads to a facetious comment about shipping Adam "back to American City"—a possible solution to their unstated problem that "had been behind, deeply in the shade," and now comes "cautiously to the front" (2:271). The final dimension is the "relief" brought to Maggie by Adam's protestation that she will "sacrifice" him only "the day you've ceased to believe in me" (2:272). Implied strongly here is that Maggie's solicitude and fears about Adam have been influenced by her unconscious suspicion that her father is a failure.

During the next part of the novel Maggie waits for the inspiration she at this point must receive before taking further action. Now her thoughts focus primarily on the relation between Charlotte and Adam, the most notorious image of which "wouldn't have been wrongly figured if he had been thought of as holding in one of his pocketed hands the end of a long silken halter looped round her beautiful neck" (2:287). One notes that this halter image is introduced by the narrator, who discerns the new element of somewhat sinister control exercised subtly but unmistakably by Adam. One should note also that the implications of the image are Maggie's Poesque "translation"—of her father's unvoiced words, for example: "Yes, you see—I lead her now by the neck, I lead her to her doom."

While watching Charlotte display the Fawns treasures to visitors, Maggie imagines Charlotte's voice sounding "like the shriek of a soul in pain." When Maggie notices Adam "across half the gallery" pondering his wife's performance, "he struck her as confessing, with strange tears in his own eyes, to sharp identity of emotion" (2:292). We observe that this is Maggie's perception; we really do not know whether or not Charlotte feels unbearable anguish. In light of subsequent events, however, we may conclude that Maggie's melodramatic imagination has combined with her propensity to identify with others to cause gross distortion. We may also conclude that her need to believe Adam is both in control yet capable of genuine sympathy has caused her to exaggerate his commiseration with his wife. At times James hints at Adam's real emotions, but, in general, his inscrutability—seemingly the major source of Adam's power—is all the reader sees.

Maggie's interpretation of her husband's behavior during this hiatus is also questionable. All we know definitely is that Amerigo is in London for part of the time, ostensibly to arrange his books. Yet Maggie's "imagination tracked him to the dusty town" and envisions him "doing penance in sordid ways." She finally decides that "he got off to escape from a sound . . . —that of Charlotte's high coerced quaver." Maggie concludes, "He had to turn away, but he wasn't at least a coward. . . . his idea could only be to wait, whatever might come, at her side" (2:294–95). James implies that this reading may be necessary, even inevitable, for Maggie during this period because it helps her to maintain "equilibrium." On the other hand, he does not invite any unequivocal conclusions about the veracity of these essentially self-serving interpretations of the behavior of either Adam, Charlotte, or Amerigo.

Just before the novel's next crucial occasion—on a boring Sunday when "one's nerves had at last done for one all that nerves could do"— Maggie worries "above all if the cord mightn't at last have snapped between her husband and her father" (2:298). She assumes also that a meeting has taken place between Charlotte and a fat Father Mitchell— "He had possibly prescribed contrition"—and that after this Charlotte has left "as a positive flight from derision." Finally, "what was clearest always in our young woman's imaginings was the sense of being herself left for any occasion in the breach. She was essentially there to bear the burden" (2:300–302). After a brief conversation with Fanny, who has guessed correctly that Adam and his wife have decided to leave England, Maggie heads out in search of Charlotte. To Maggie at this point, Charlotte has become like "Io goaded by the gadfly" or "Ariadne roaming the lone sea-strand."[17] To herself, Maggie "might have been for the hour some far-off harassed heroine—only with a part to play for which she knew exactly no inspiring precedent." Maggie does know, however, that she wishes to find Charlotte and "make somehow, for her support, the last demonstration" (2:307). As several of these phrases suggest, Maggie's hermeneutic is probably exaggerated. On the other hand, given the passage of time, the slow movement of events, her separation from her husband, and her ambivalence about Charlotte, Maggie's state of mind is understandable.

The brief scene in the "ancient rotunda" away from the house has a peculiar tone—portentous and yet somehow comic. The comedy derives, first of all, from the attitudes already referred to with which Maggie, clutching her parasol and a novel for Charlotte, sallies forth to supply imagined succor. The tone derives as well from the stance that Maggie takes up upon meeting Charlotte and from the imagery by which Maggie figures her approach: she reminds "herself really of people she had read about in stories of the wild west, people who threw up their hands on certain occasions as a sign they weren't carrying revolvers" (2:310–11). The comedy derives, finally, from the "part" that Charlotte is "more or less visibly in possession of" and from the words she flings at Maggie: "I'm tired . . ."; "Tired of this life—the one we've been leading. You like it, I know, but I've dreamed another dream"; "How I see . . . that you've worked against me!" And so on (2:313–18).

Maggie is tremendously impressed by Charlotte, "splendid and erect," and she labors hard to help her maintain her stance and spit out her dialogue. Yet undercutting Charlotte's impressiveness is James's parody of the role she quite consciously acts out: that of the wronged, virtuous heroine of a romantic play. Complicating the tone are the irony and pathos deriving from the role Maggie eagerly takes on—with a constant effort "still to follow the right line." In her rendering, Maggie becomes by the bittersweet conclusion the scheming villainess, justly punished for her nefarious but unrepentant ways.

Several critics who are not convinced that Maggie's experience improves her morally mention her failure to admit responsibility for her marriage problems. It is true that, very near the end of the novel, she says to Fanny that it is "just, it's right, it's deserved" that Charlotte and Amerigo are "lost to each other" whereas "for us it's only sad and strange and not caused by our own fault" (2:333). Yet twice before, as has been mentioned, she acknowledges her failings. Moreover, in a scene such as the one just analyzed, she evinces at least subconscious guilt in the eagerness with which in "secret responsive ecstasy" she accepts her "supreme abjection" (2:313) in front of Charlotte. One might argue also that her excessive concern for Charlotte's pain just prior to the leave-taking also suggests guilt she cannot acknowledge openly.[18] That James knows this is suggested by his narrative comment: "This imagined service to the woman who could no longer help herself was one of the traps set for Maggie's spirit at every turn of the road" (2:330).

The Wages of Virtue

James's tough-minded refusal to sentimentalize either Maggie's display of goodness or the results of it is clearly shown in the last book of *The Golden Bowl.* Its first important occasion begins with a telegram from Charlotte that has caused Maggie to visit Amerigo's room—to her a "locked cage." Immediately, she is assaulted by "an extraordinary fact. . . . He was with her as if he were hers, hers in a degree and on a scale, with an intensity and an intimacy, that were a new and strange quality, that were like the irruption of a tide loosening them where they had stuck and making them feel they floated" (2:339–40).

The Princess protects herself with talk of the Verver departure, suggestions about a decorous meeting between Amerigo and Charlotte, and a perception of Charlotte "in pain . . . in torment." The Prince refers to Maggie's "value"; then he disparages Charlotte: "She doesn't know you now"; "she understands you ever so much less." Finally, the Prince "abruptly opined, 'She's stupid.' "[19] But after Maggie's "long wail" informs him dramatically that he has erred, Amerigo backs down: "what I mean is that she's not, as you perceive her, unhappy" (2:347–48).

As the conversation continues and Maggie maintains her sympathy, the Prince says, "She won't let you take her for unhappy," and then, "Everything's terrible, cara—in the heart of man." At last he says, with some impatience, "She's making her life. She'll make it" (2:349). What seems to happen is that the Prince, attracted by the fight Maggie has put up for him, bored by the position his infidelity has plunged him into, aware of his financial dependence upon Maggie's millions, and—in all probability—not having been close to Charlotte in several weeks, tries indirectly and without losing face to tell his wife he cares more about her than his former mistress. When he discovers that his brusque comments wound Maggie, he tries to smooth things over; then he becomes impatient and says, in effect: This is what life is like, don't worry about Charlotte, she's a survivor and will look after herself.

Perhaps the only thing really surprising about the scene's next few moments is Maggie's continued unwillingness to give in to an extremely potent sexual attraction: "He was so near now that she could touch him, taste him, smell him, kiss him, hold him" (2:352). Her self-control, however, should not be condemned; in fact, she should probably be applauded because she knows that she might later regret any surrender made now. Thus, the last line of the chapter might be spoken by both Maggie and the narrator: "She had saved herself and she got off" (2:353).

After Charlotte and Adam arrive and Charlotte and Amerigo seat themselves for tea, Adam and his daughter compliment each other with soothing statements about their success: "It's all right, eh? Oh, my dear—rather!" (2:359). At the same time their eyes roam the room, in search of exquisite objects deserving of "recognition and applause," to which "general harmony" the Prince and Charlotte contribute: "Mrs. Verver and the Prince fairly 'placed' themselves, however unwittingly, as high expressions of the kind of human furniture required aesthetically by such a scene." The narrator speaks of how they add to the "triumph of selection" symbolized by this meeting, and that "they also might have figured as concrete attestations of a rare power of purchase" (2:360).

Whether it is "selection" (which implies taste and care) or "power of purchase" (which implies only money), the implications here are pejorative. James understands the resonances of his novel very well: there is instrumentalism in the relation of Adam and Maggie to their respective spouses. On the other hand, they care, genuinely and even passionately, about their furniture. Given this fact it is perhaps cheering that Adam agrees to Maggie's categorization of Charlotte as "incomparable," "great" (2:363–64).

Later Maggie is impressed by the note of "possession and control" (2:365) when Adam speaks about his wife. Again, readers may not admire this attitude; it is nonetheless consistent with her revealed need to see her father as successful. She also must, because of the pain caused by Charlotte and perhaps because of a continued fear, believe she has been put in her place. At the same time, if we are disturbed by this residue of selfishness, James indicates that this is only a small part of her character: she appreciates Charlotte's "gifts, her variety, her power"; moreover, she does not want these gifts to be hidden or frittered away. Thus, she feels pleasure when she thinks, "Great for the world that was before her—*that* he proposed she should be; she wasn't to be wasted in the application of his plan" (2:365–66). This attitude is not selfish; it is high and generous.

After Adam and Charlotte leave, the Prince and Maggie are left alone and Maggie becomes vividly aware of "her reason for what she had done." Now, in language mingling the romantic and puritanical—for James a quintessentially American mixture—the narrator speaks of Maggie knowing "really why—and how she had been inspired and guided, how she had been persistently able, how to her soul all the while it had been for the sake of this end. Here it was then, the moment, the golden fruit that had shone from afar." The golden bowl without the crack is at hand, the amount is to be "paid," the "dice" (2:367) will reveal their winning numbers. Quite naturally, as she moves to experience this moment, she "had an instant of terror"; quite naturally as she responds to Amerigo's "presence alone," her momentary terror turns to a feeling of "safety." And, given her general need to experience others at their best and her particular need to encounter Amerigo at his most attractive, quite natural also is her "concern for his own anxiety, for everything that was deep in his being and everything that was fair in his face" (2:368).

Finally, when these other needs and desires are combined with Maggie's respect for Charlotte, quite natural is her "new horror" that Amerigo will "confess" to her—will assume, in fact, she expects a "confession." If it comes it will come "at the expense of Charlotte"; thus to prevent words Maggie would be "ashamed" to hear, she speaks positively of her friend. Charlotte is "splendid"; "That's our help, you see," Maggie says, "to point further her moral." But now Amerigo tries "too clearly, to please her—to meet her in her own way." Moreover, his presence is "enclosing her" until finally he says, "See? I see nothing but *you*" (2:368–69).

Maggie is convinced from the previous signs and from a new one—a look that "strangely lighted his eyes"—that Amerigo is being truthful: she has won back her husband, for the time, totally. Although by now the narrator is no longer certain of Maggie's response to the epiphany, he guesses she will feel "pity and dread" (2:369) of what the eyes may say to her. There may be pity for Charlotte, who has been so completely obliterated; pity perhaps for Amerigo—deriving from Maggie's sudden not fully understood sense of the dependent state to which her actions have driven him. There may be "dread" for the responsibility these actions and Amerigo's reaction have thrust upon her—the continual, arguably heroic need to bring high gloss to the gilt bowl of her marriage. Maggie wanted her husband; now she has him. She knows, however, it will not be easy to keep his love. And the reader knows that, to be successful, Maggie must live by a complex, continually changing code of goodness.[20]

Chapter Nine
Conclusion

Although during the slightly more than a decade after he completed *The Golden Bowl* James finished no novels, his record of accomplishment is outstanding, particularly in view of his health problems, from which he was seldom free. He published first his impressions as "restless analyst" of the United States; these were formed between August 1904 and July 1905, during his stimulating, controversial, exhausting, and extremely public American tour. After revision and inclusion of new material, the articles became the penetrating 1907 travel book, *The American Scene.*[1]

During the visit to America James also revealed a new side of his literary personality: not only did he grant interviews to the press but he also delivered more than twenty lucrative, well-attended lectures in various cities—the majority on "The Lesson of Balzac," a few on "The Question of Our Speech" (whose criticism of "the slipshod ways in which American girls spoke"[2] was, as Leon Edel points out, frequently interpreted as evidence of James's attack on the American language). James during the tour did not metamorphose into Mark Twain; in general, however, his beautifully organized, elegantly conversational lectures were well received by auditors who welcomed the respect shown for their intelligence and sensitivity. (Later in England, in the spring of 1912, he would again lecture successfully—on his former neighbor at De Vere Gardens, Robert Browning; James's topic at this centenary celebration was "The Novel in *The Ring and the Book.*")

Extremely significant during this period was James's creation of the twenty-four volume New York Edition of his short stories, novellas, and novels. Much of his time between late 1905 and 1909 was devoted to revising the majority of his fiction and to writing the eighteen uniquely informative prefaces. Since so many references have already been made to this magnificent edition, little more needs to be said. It should be stressed, however, that, contrary to the scholarly consensus, James did not regard this edition exclusively—perhaps even primarily—as a means by which he could achieve wide intelligent recognition and, ultimately, literary immortality. He viewed the edition as in part a commercial enterprise,[3] evidence of whose failure helped devastate him, perhaps causing a nervous breakdown in early 1910. The image of James projected throughout this study, therefore, of a man who consistently tried to juggle aesthetic and financial considerations, is enhanced by his experience with the New York Edition. Moreover, as with the failure of many specific novels to find a wide audience, James here took only tepid solace from the adulation of his friends (Morton Fullerton, for example, who wrote a fulsome review), or from his success in completing a task according to exacting artistic standards.

While James, with waning enthusiasm, was finishing his collected edition, he reimmersed himself in the world of the theater, enticed again by its excitement, and chance for large financial gain and public recognition, and also the mood of the time, which encouraged dramatic experimentation. In late 1907 Johnston Forbes-Robertson asked James to turn his short story "Covering End," written in 1895 as a one-act play, into a comedy for himself and his wife. As a result, James wrote theatrical material sporadically for two years. For Forbes-Robertson, he created *The High Bid,* a three-act comedy of manners about an American lady who helps save an English estate from the indifference of its radical owner and from a rich American, who yearns to purchase it. After the play had been unsuccessful on the road, Forbes-Robertson eventually discharged his obligation to James by performing the comedy in London at five matinees.[4]

James also wrote the one-act "The Saloon," intended to be a curtain raiser for *The High Bid* and adapted from the short story "Owen Wingrave," about a young pacifist who proves his bravery by remaining the night, and dying, in a haunted house. The drama was later rejected by the Incorporated Stage Society, which included George Bernard Shaw. (Shaw probably would have backed producing "The Saloon" if James had changed the ending so that the hero vanquished the ghost; the novelist, however, refused the request.) As well, James turned his novella, *The Other House,* back into the Ibsenesque melodrama it had been originally when written in the 1890s. Finally, he wrote a new play, *The Outcry,* intended to be performed in repertory along with dramas by Galsworthy, Shaw, J. M. Barrie, and Harley Granville-Barker in the summer of 1910. Although the death of King Edward closed the theaters and, as a result, James's comedy about the attempt of an

American to buy English art treasures was not performed, he received $1,000 for the script; moreover, he almost immediately turned it into a novella, which became surprisingly popular.

James sailed to America because of illness in the summer of 1910. Soon after, in August, his brother William died. Then, about a year later, after returning to England, James began an ostensible biography of his famous sibling—a project, however, that soon became an auto-biographical portrait of the author as a young observer, *A Small Boy and Others*. This book was followed by a volume somewhat more bio-graphical in intent—*Notes of a Son and Brother*. That its genre was also autobiography, however, was evinced by its impressionistic structure, its distinctive narrative voice, and its selection of materials (such as the elegiac reminiscences about the impact of the vibrant Minny Temple's death upon the young, incipient novelist). During much of the time between fall 1911 and fall 1913, James dictated this conversational re-creation of his personal past.

James's other important completed books are his collections of short fiction, *The Finer Grain* (1910), and criticism, *Notes on Novelists* (1914). Each of the five stories in *The Finer Grain* was published separately in either 1909 or 1910. Close thematic links between the stories—par-ticularly in the treatment of the power of the artistic imagination—suggest that, in the volume, James was consciously trying to create a quasi-novelistic short-story cycle (anticipating Joyce's *Dubliners*).[5] Al-though most material for *Notes on Novelists* was written prior to 1904, two significant exceptions were James's essay on Balzac and his article about the contemporary novel, "The Younger Generation," which ap-peared in two installments in the *Times Literary Supplement* in the spring of 1914. Leon Edel writes that "All the English novelists of the day read the article and many felt themselves ignored; the Master, undis-turbed, had had his say."[6]

James's final completed literary project was also an act of criticism and appreciation—a long, sympathetic preface to Rupert Brooke's *Let-ters from America*. The young poet, whom James had met and whose attractiveness had overwhelmed him during a June 1909 visit to Cam-bridge undergraduates, had died of blood poisoning in the summer of 1914, after service with the British navy. James welcomed the request to contribute to this publication.

With respect to projects begun but left unfinished at James's death, three are worthy of brief discussion. The first is a book about London, contracted for before his American tour. James's *Notebooks* tell us of his attempt to gather material through visiting evocative locations in both late summer 1907 and 1909; nothing survives of the project, however, even though Macmillan commissioned etchings by the illustrator, Joseph Pennell, who talked to James upon his return from America and who completed his work by the spring of 1908. After examining the many apparently unread pages of historical books about London belonging to James, John Kimmey has conjectured that the novelist did not complete his volume because he "did not possess the requisite historical background or interest."[7] The past for James was primarily old objects or places surviving into the present, important because they stimulated poignant impressions.

During these years, James also began two (or three, depending upon one's point of view) projects that, if completed, might have led to novels. One was begun in the *Notebooks* in late 1909 and referred to first as the "K. B. Case" and later "Mrs. Max." James started to develop the "Mrs. Max" notes after several months of writing for the theater and after being asked by F. W. Duneka, a Harper's editor, for a new 100,000-word serial on an American subject. Illness, however, halted the plan, which was held further in abeyance by William's death and James's work on autobiography. Then, as a result of some well-intentioned conniving by Edith Wharton, he was asked by Charles Scribner, in the fall of 1912, for an American novel. James never discovered that the request and the generous financial terms offered by Scribner had been engineered by Wharton, who, imagining her friend to be destitute, asked the publisher to advance James money from her large account.

After some initial reluctance, James pocketed the substantial advance ($3,600) and later (some time in 1914) began a book that seemingly drew most of its inspiration from his visits to America in 1904–5 and 1910–11 (although a few names were appropriated from the "Mrs. Max" project). If James had finished *The Ivory Tower* it might have been, as several scholars have predicted, a major novel about the evils of American capitalism. But "might have been" should be emphasized: the book is unfinished (three books and the first chapter of a fourth were drafted); the notes are tentative.[8] We really do not know in what direction the plot would have gone or what attitude—to mention an area of critical disagreement—we as readers would have been invited to take toward its anti-materialistic protagonist, Graham Fielder, or his deceptive friend, Horton Vint, who mishandles Gray's inheritance.

The notes suggest James's original eagerness to create sections named after and centering around particular characters, and structured like acts in a play (as in *The Awkward Age,* which James mentions). As the notes proceed, however, he encounters several problems about which he at times speaks confidently, but at others seems uneasy or confused: about the danger, for example, of making one character (Cissy Foy) too similar to Charlotte Stant of *The Golden Bowl*; about how certain characters (Cissy and Rosanna Gaw, for example) are to relate plausibly to the action and about their relative importance to it; about how his somewhat hazy memory of America could be used to create settings other than "the only place known to me in the country" (354)—Newport, Rhode Island—as well as modern artifacts like "cars and telephones . . . and resources of certain sorts" (which, James remarks, "I can't not take account of" [355–56]); about the "enormous difficulty of pretending to show various things here as with a business vision, in my total absence of business initiation" (293); about how to reconcile his love of the scenic method with the need to filter large sections of the action through Graham Fielder's consciousness.

More generally, the notes suggest James's doubts about his ability to write a novel. Could he still nail together the boards of a large house of fiction without compromising too much—or even destroying—the architectural principles it was intended to embody: the "magnificent masterly little vivid economy" (278), the "magnificent packed and calculated closeness" (347), the "cherished symmetry and unity" (349)— the "lucidity *with* the complexity" (348)?

James had not written a novel for approximately a decade, during which his narrative constructions had been relatively short and uncomplicated. In composing his long projects (*The American Scene* and the autobiographical books, for example) he had indulged in the blessed "fluidity of the first-person form." (He implies in the preface to *The Ambassadors* that the fluidity becomes "terrible" in the novel—a genre intended to be unified, economical, and intense.) Now, almost at the end of his life, James confronted again in the idea for *The Ivory Tower* the exhilarating but also potentially exhausting challenges of the art of the novel. Although the scholarly consensus is that James put aside the manuscript because, with the outbreak of war in August, 1914, he could not "work upon a fiction supposed to represent contemporary or recent life" (v), a more likely reason is lack of artistic confidence.

Certainly no reluctance about contemporary life prevented him from thrilling to stories about the war (despite his occasional profound sadness), from visiting wounded soldiers, from acting as honorary chairman of the American Volunteer Motor-Ambulance Corps in France, from writing sensitive letters to the parents of dead soldiers, from applying for and gaining British citizenship on 28 July 1915. Nor did reluctance prevent him from completing the lengthy preface to Rupert Brooke's posthumous *Letters from America,* which James seems to have begun after abandoning *The Ivory Tower* and which he finished in November 1915.

The scholarly consensus about James's reason for beginning his last would-be novel—a story about time travel, *The Sense of the Past*—is also that he wanted to escape the grim reality of war. Perhaps so, but another possible reason was his hope that, after his exercise with the recalcitrant *Ivory Tower,* he might now successfully confront this new challenge. James had first begun *The Sense of the Past* fifteen years previously, in 1900, after he had been asked by F. N. Doubleday, an editor at Harper's, for a ghost story resembling the recently published and popular *Turn of the Screw.* In response to this request (and a somewhat later one from William Dean Howells for an "international ghost") James devised a plot about an American amateur historian, Ralph Pendrell—criticized for his passivity and infatuation with Europe by the woman he loves, Aurora Coyne—who voyages to London to inspect a house inherited from a distant cousin. Upon arriving, Ralph notices a portrait of a handsome young ancestor, begins to think the subject is alive, and then that the face is his own. Eventually, Ralph trades temporal places with this alter ego from 1820. James laid his pages aside so that he could write *The Ambassadors* and did not look at them seriously again until, after coming to London in the fall of 1915, he asked his secretary to return to Rye, locate the manuscript, and deliver it to him.

James focused on *The Sense of the Past* for several weeks, during which he revised the opening and also dictated notes that were much less tentative and probably more satisfying than the notes for *The Ivory Tower.* Particularly pleasurable seems to have been his ability to solve (at least in theory) the problems that emerged continually as he worked his way through the plot and emerged at the end with Ralph safely back in 1910 London, engaged in a hypothetical closing scene with the American ambassador. This occasion would not only balance an earlier one but also avoid "The comparatively platitudinous direct *duo* between the parties [Ralph and Aurora]" (358).[9]

Late in his dictation of this quite complete scenario, James exclaimed, "What a blessing thus to find, accordingly, how the old gentle firmness of pressure, piously applied, doesn't fail to supply me" (353). In his euphoria at creating again the preliminaries to a novel, James temporarily forgot that his plot depended to a very large extent upon "romantic hocuspocus" (336)—the adoration of Ralph and the sacrifice on his behalf by an 1820 Cinderella figure, for example. On the other hand, in its romantic and melodramatic beginnings, *The Sense of the Past* does not differ greatly from many James novels.

A crucial difference, however, is that *The Sense of the Past* was not allowed to benefit from the "intimacy of composition." As James wrote in the notes to *The Ivory Tower,* during composition "prenoted arrangements, proportions and relations, do most uncommonly insist on making themselves different by shifts and variations, always improving, which impose themselves as one goes and keep the door open always to something *more* right and *more* related" (350). Unfortunately, in this instance, the Master could not be mastered by this mysterious process because he was conquered by death: James's first stroke came early in the morning of 2 December 1915. As he lapsed into confusion and bizarre Napoleonic dictations, successful negotiations brought him in late December the Order of Merit, awarded hitherto to only George Meredith and Thomas Hardy.

When Henry James died on 28 February 1916, he was not quite seventy-three years old. Despite his failure to complete his last two novels, he had published superb nonfiction and fiction for over fifty years; in so doing, he had produced a body of work that, arguably, was then and is still the greatest and most influential ever written by an American.

Notes and References

The first note for each of the main chapters provides a selective list of relevant criticism in English published after 1970, and is divided into books, essays discussing revisions, and general essays. Entries on most essays are bibliographically complete. References to a few essays, however, and to many discussions in books are given in short form; comprehensive bibliographical information is provided in the selected bibliography, under secondary sources.

For scholarship prior to 1970, readers should consult Robert Gale's concise survey in *Eight American Authors*, ed. James Woodress (New York, 1971), 321–75, and the very thorough "Checklist," compiled by Maurice Beebe and William Stafford Jr., in *Modern Fiction Studies* 12 (1966):112–77.

For additional information, readers should consult Kristan Pruitt McColgan, ed., *Henry James, 1917–59: A Reference Guide* (Boston, 1979); Dorothy McInnis Scara, ed., *Henry James, 1960–74: A Reference Guide* (Boston, 1980); John Budd, comp. *Henry James: A Bibliography of Criticism, 1975–81* (Westport, Conn., 1983); and Beatrice Ricks, ed., *Henry James: A Bibliography of Secondary Works* (Metuchen, N. J., 1975).

For evaluative discussions of the scholarship on James, readers should peruse the annual articles about it appearing in *American Literary Scholarship*, published by Duke University Press, and in the *Henry James Review*.

Specific texts cited in this book are identified in the notes. New York editions of the novels have usually been selected; the exceptions are the *The Ambassadors* and *The Wings of the Dove*, where the Norton Critical Edition has been chosen. For each choice, an explanation is provided.

Preface

1. Leon Edel, ed. *Henry James Letters, vol. 4: 1895–1916* (Cambridge, Mass., 1984), 367–68.

Chapter One

1. Reprinted in R. Gard, ed., *Henry James: The Critical Heritage* (London, 1968), 141; hereafter cited in the text.

2. James was always very conscious of sales, even after his theatrical failure (1895) when, according to most critics, he decided to write for fit audience though few.

Chapter Two

1. *The Princess Casamassima,* New York Edition, vols. 5–6 (New York, 1908), 1:v; hereafter cited in the text. This edition is considered definitive and is used in virtually all reprints.

For secondary literature see the following.

Books entirely on *Princess*: W. Tilley, *The Background of The Princess Casamassima* (Gainesville, Fla., 1960).

Books that include discussion of *Princess*: P. Buitenhuis, *The Grasping Imagination* (Toronto, 1970), 160–65; P. Dolan, *Of War and War's Alarms* (New York, 1976), 4–7, 70–95; R. Gill, *Happy Rural Seat* (New Haven, 1972), 56–62; M. Jacobson, *Henry James* (University, Ala., 1983) 41–61; P. Keating, *The Working Classes in Victorian Fiction* (London, 1971), 46–52; C. Maves, *Sensuous Pessimism* (Bloomington, 1973), 83–87; J. O'Neill, *Workable Design* (Port Washington, N.Y., 1973), 49–69; S. Perosa, *Henry James* (Charlottesville, 1978), 26–34; J. Rowe, *The Theoretical Dimensions of Henry James* (Madison, 1984), 147–88; C. Samuels, *The Ambiguity of Henry James* (Urbana, 1971), 50–60; M. Seltzer, *Henry James* (Ithaca, 1984), 18–21, 27–58; P. Sicker, *Love and the Quest for Identity* (Princeton, 1980), 64–72; D. Stone, *Novelists in a Changing World* (Cambridge, Mass., 1972) 283–308, W. Stowe, *Balzac, James, and the Realistic Novel* (Princeton, 1983) 56–99.

Essays discussing revisions: H. Girling, "On Editing a Paragraph of *The Princess Casamassima,*" *Language and Style* 8 (1975):243–63.

General essays: M. Banta, "Beyond Post-Modernism: The Sense of History in *The Princess Casamassima,*" *Henry James Review* 3 (1982):96–107; J. Barstow, "Originality and Conventionality in *The Princess Casamassima,*" *Genre* 11 (1978):445–58; J. Cox, "Henry James," *Southern Review* 8, n.s. (1972):493–506; M. Faber, "Henry James: Revolutionary Involvement, the Princess, and the Hero," *American Imago* 37 (1980):245–77; J. Kimmey, "*The Tragic Muse* and Its Forerunners," *American Literature* 41 (1969–70):518–31; M. Lay, "The Real Beasts: Surrogate Brothers in James's 'The Pupil' and *The Princess Casamassima,*" *American Literary Realism* 13 (1980):73–84; B. Richards, "Another Model for Christina Light," *Henry James Review* 5 (1983):60–65; D. Seed, "Hyacinth Robinson and the Politics of *The Princess Casamassima,*" *Etudes Anglaise* 30 (1977):30–39; T. Stoehr, "Words and Deeds in *The Princess Casamassima,*" *ELH* 37 (1970):95–135; A. Tintner, "Keats and James in *The Princess Casamassima,*" *Nineteenth Century Fiction* 28 (1973–74):179–93.

2. L. Edel, ed. *Henry James Letters,* vol. 3:1883–95 (Cambridge, Mass., 1980), 89. *Letters,* 3:61.

3. F. Matthiessen and K. Murdock, eds., *The Notebooks of Henry James* (Oxford, 1961), 68.

4. *Letters,* 3:134. James's lamentations about the length of his works echo throughout this period—in part, one suspects, because this complaint was made repeatedly by critics on both sides of the Atlantic who disliked his fiction: not only were James's books dull and pessimistic, but they were also dull, pessimistic, and long.

5. For information about the critical reception of James's works see in particular, Gard, ed., *Henry James,* and L. Taylor, *Henry James, 1866–1916: A Reference Guide* (Boston, 1982).

6. For a discussion of the collaboration see C. Higgins, "Photographic Aperture: Coburn's Frontispieces to James's New York Edition," *American Literature* 53 (1982):661–75. There is no reliable published study of James's revisions for the New York Edition of *The Princess.* Frederick Nies's recently completed South Carolina dissertation is, however, according to the *Henry James Review* "the most detailed and comprehensive study to date of James's revisions."

7. For the many critics who believe *The Princess Casamassima* to be a "transitional" novel, the major difference between James's handling of Hyacinth and most of the early observer-narrators is that, after the first few chapters of the novel, James sees the action with relative consistency from his protagonist's perspective (although not as consistently as with Strether in *The Ambassadors* or Fleda Vetch in *The Spoils of Poynton,* for example).

8. Émile Zola, *Germinal,* trans. E. Vizetelly (London, 1925), 356.

Chapter Three

1. *Letters,* 3:133–34.

For secondary literature see the following.

Books: R. Blackmur, *Studies in Henry James,* ed. Veronica A. Makowsky (New York, 1983), 202–12; D. Fogel, *Henry James* (Baton Rouge, 1981), 172–74; J. Goode, ed., *The Air of Reality* (London, 1972), 81–167; K. Graham, *Henry James* (London, 1975), 79–126; Jacobson, *Henry James,* 62–80; Perosa, *Henry James,* 38–43; R. Posnock, *Henry James* (Athens, Georgia, 1985); L. Powers, *Henry James* (Lansing, Mich.), 124–63; Stone, *Novelists,* 170–71, 308–30; E. Wagenknecht, *Eve and Henry James* (Norman, Okla., 1978) 73–90; E. Wagenknecht, *The Novels of Henry James* (New York, 1983), 119–33; V. Winner, *Henry James* (Charlottesville, 1970), 118–26.

Essays discussing revisions: T. Leitch, "The Editor as Hero: Henry James and the New York Edition," *Henry James Review* 3 (1981):30.

General essays: R. Baker, "Gabriel Nash's 'House of Strange Idols': Aestheticism in *The Tragic Muse*," *Texas Studies in Literature and Language* 15 (1973):149–66; J. Funston, " 'All Art Is One': Narrative Techniques in Henry James's *The Tragic Muse*," *Studies in the Novel* 15 (1983):344–55; W. Goetz, "The Allegory of Representation in *The Tragic Muse*," *Journal of Narrative Technique* 8 (1978):151–64; D. Schneider, "The Theme of Freedom in James's *The Tragic Muse*," *Connecticut Review* 7 (1974):5–15.

2. In the introduction to *Henry James*, Gard argues that *The Tragic Muse* "both in sales and in many of its British reviews, was the nadir of James's career as a novelist. . . . Its reception forced on him the full consciousness of how little interest there was in his work. And it had immediate consequences in determining him to devote himself (1890–95) to writing plays for the commercial theatre" (12). Gard exaggerates here because the causes of James's decision to write for the theater are complex and, as the many positive American reviews excerpted by Linda Taylor in *Henry James* (Boston, 1982) suggest, *The Tragic Muse* was relatively well received in the United States (a few reviewers believed it to be his best novel). On the other hand, *The Tragic Muse* did not sell as well as he had hoped, and James was bothered by this fact.

3. The sources for the dramatic plot most frequently and convincingly cited are William Black's *Macleod of Dare*, which James had reviewed for the *Nation* in 1878, and his friend Mrs. Humphry Ward's *Miss Bretherton*.

4. Funston, in " 'All Art is One,' " exaggerates James's dissatisfaction with *The Tragic Muse*. Initially, he was embarrassed by its length, but this problem bothered him with much of his fiction. In his preface he seems most disappointed by his treatment of Nick Dormer, but his overall impression of the novel is positive.

5. The word "beastly" was added to the New York Edition. Although at times Nash is maddeningly cool in his responses to life, the novelist tries in scenes such as this to suggest strongly that a part of Nash can be touched and hurt.

6. While expatiating on the pleasure he hopes to derive from encouraging Nick to change careers, Nash exclaims, "Perfidious wretch, you're capable of having talent—which of course will spoil everything" (1:183). The significant change from the 1890 text is the addition of the final subordinate clause, which anticipates and partially explains Nash's waning of interest in Nick after Nick's talent as a portrait painter creates in him a need to work.

7. This, and subsequent references, are to Blackmur's Dell Laurel reprint (New York, 1961) of the 1890 text.

Chapter Four

1. A. Margolis, in *Henry James* (Ann Arbor, 1985), suggests that another reason for James's move to the theater was the oppressive atmosphere of censorship in the world of fiction, perhaps best illustrated by the campaign of the National Vigilance Association to suppress English translations of French naturalists. The subject was debated in Parliament in May 1888 and,

after two trials, Zola's publisher, Henry Vizetelly, was eventually jailed for three months.

2. Although James completed the play ("Summersoft") quickly, when he delivered it to Ellen Terry she had already acquired another vehicle. James then turned the play into a short story ("Covering End") and published it along with *The Turn of the Screw* in *The Two Magics.*

3. Three scholars have written books devoted to the supposed influence of James's experience in the theater on his subsequent fiction, particularly that written between 1896 and 1901: M. Egan, *Henry James: The Ibsen Years,* W. Isle, *Experiments in Form* (Cambridge, Mass., 1968), and J. Wiesenfarth, *Henry James and The Dramatic Analogy* (New York, 1963). For other substantial discussions of this subject see Lawrence Holland, *The Expense of Vision* (Princeton, 1964), 57–119; Jacobson, *Henry James,* 100–138; Margolis, *Henry James,* 97–136; Perosa, *Henry James,* 45–76; J. Ward, *The Search for Form* (Chapel Hill, 1967), 28–59, 141–63.

4. Quoted in *Henry James: Selected Literary Criticism,* ed. Morris Shapira (London, 1963), 211.

5. Although there are many excellent studies of James's late style, readers should consult, in particular, S. Chatman, *The Later Style of Henry James* (New York, 1972); R. Normann, *The Insecure World of Henry James's Fiction* (London, 1982); I. Watt, "The First Paragraph of *The Ambassadors*: An Explication," *Essays in Criticism* 10 (1960):250–74; and R. Yeazell, *Language and Knowledge* (Chicago, 1976).

Chapter Five

1. For secondary literature see the following.

Books: W. Isle, *Experiments in Form* (Cambridge, Mass., 1968), 165–204; Jacobson, *Henry James,* 121–38; S. Moore, *The Drama of Discrimination in Henry James* (St. Lucia, 1982), 79–109; O'Neill, *Workable Design,* 87–104; Perosa, *Henry James,* 68–74; S. Purdy, *The Hole in the Fabric* (Pittsburgh, 1977), 132–49; Samuels, *Ambiguity* 150–77; Sicker, *Love,* 85–99; Wagenknecht, *Eve,* 134–52; Wagenknecht, *Novels,* 32–33, 162–69; Goode, ed., 190–218.

General essays: J. Blackall, "The Case for Mrs. Brook," *Henry James Review* 2 (1981):155–61; J. Blackall, "Literary Allusion as Imaginative Event in *The Awkward Age,*" *Modern Fiction Studies* 26 (1980):177–97; S. Culver, "Censorship and Intimacy: Awkwardness in *The Awkward Age,*" *ELH* 48 (1981):368–86; A. Davidson, "James's Dramatic Method in *The Awkward Age,*" *Nineteenth Century Fiction* 29 (1974):320–35; F. Gillen, "The Dramatist in His Drama: Theory versus Effect in *The Awkward Age,*" *Texas Studies in Literature and Language* 12 (1971):663–74; E. Owen, "*The Awkward Age* and the Contemporary English Scene," *Victorian Studies* 11 (1967):63–82; E. Sklepowich, "Gilded Bondage: Games and Gamesplaying in *The Awkward Age,*" *Essays in Literature* 5 (1978):187–93; D. Schneider, "James's *The Awkward*

Age: A Reading and an Evaluation," *Henry James Review* 1 (1980):215–226; T. Todorov, "The Verbal Age," trans. P. Gibby, *Critical Inquiry* 4 (1977):351–71.

2. It is almost impossible to generalize about the critical responses to the novel: some readers hated it and objected to its coldness, obscurity, length, and immorality (as well as to a "James cult" that helped keep his books in print); others admired it and praised James's style, satirical gift, and subtlety.

3. *The Awkward Age,* New York Edition, vol. 9 (New York, 1908), 333; hereafter cited in the text.

4. Edel argues that James's many portrayals of children during this period are related to his "personal healing process" after his failure in the theater, and that his fiction about children embodies "an extensive personal allegory of the growing up of Henry James" (see *The Treacherous Years* [New York, 1969], 260–65). A significant source of James's focus on young people during the 1890s was his occasional repugnance and fear—revealed frequently in his letters—about the vulgarity of English values: children would suffer severely from adult selfishness and immorality. Certainly the most poignant sections of several James stories are ones in which children (Maisie, for example) are compelled to assume quasi-parental roles.

5. See *Notebooks,* 191–92.

6. For example, dialogue novels by James's friends E. F. Benson and Violet Hunt. Jacobson suggests that the form's popularity "may account for the willingness with which *Harper's Weekly* agreed to run *The Awkward Age*" (*Henry James,* 123).

7. See P. Lubbock, ed., *The Letters of Henry James,* vol. 1 (New York, 1920), 289.

8. Many critics stress the objectivity of James's form and support James's own contention that he did not "go behind" his characters. Gillen, however, argues convincingly that "James is more interested in controlling reader response than in that 'objectivity' which is so often attributed to him" ("The Dramatist," 673).

9. Some critics observe in the novel a satire intended to expose the shady values of the London set and its cynosure, Mrs. Brook. More idiosyncratic readings reverse the point of the satire: Nanda and Longdon are smug, puritanical hypocrites; whereas the activities of the London group are essentially life-affirming—a more or less joyous creation of hedonistic supreme fictions. Other critics observe in James's treatment of Mrs. Brook critical awareness and rueful admiration, and in his handling of Nanda and Longdon nostalgic sympathy and respect occasionally undercut by skepticism.

10. Just as Nanda prepares to visit Longdon, Mrs. Brook says, " 'And what day can you go if *I* want?' Mrs. Brook spoke as with a small sharpness—just softened indeed in time—produced by the sight of a freedom in her daughter's life that suddenly loomed larger than any freedom of her own"

(327–28). Here one also notes James's willingness as narrator to clarify the motive of his character.

11. Sicker, on the other hand, argues that Nanda's relationship with Van is "overtly narcissistic" and that she loves Van because he could "love her only as the pure image that she longs to be" (*Love,* 92).

12. Owen, *"The Awkward Age,"* mentions James's knowledge (through his friend, Edmund Gosse) of John Addington Symonds' defense of homosexuality, the privately printed pamphlet *A Problem in Modern Ethics* (1891).

13. Mitchy asks, "A final irrevocable flight with him is the line he advises, so that he'll be ready for it on the spot with the post-chaise and the pistols?" (525). And later, Longdon himself refers to their "trysting-place" (531). Although the imagery seems ironic, it also hints at real, suppressed feelings.

14. Occasional hints link Mitchy's frustration (despair is probably not too strong a word) to his unreciprocated longing for Van. He refers to Van as "Apollo" (126), for example.

15. Henry James, *The Awkward Age* (London, 1899), 373.

16. The narrator also—in a sardonic reporting of Van's thoughts—has Van ask himself, "what that she [Nanda] could ever do for him would really be so beautiful as this present chance to smooth his confusion and add as much as possible to that refined satisfaction with himself which would proceed from his having dealt with a difficult hour in a gallant and delicate way?" (501).

Chapter Six

1. S. Rosenbaum, ed., *The Ambassadors* (New York, 1964), 405; hereafter cited in the text.

For secondary literature see the following.

Critical editions: F. Dupee, ed., *The Ambassadors* (New York, Rinehart, 1972); A. Kazin, ed., *The Ambassadors* (Toronto; Bantam, 1969); and Rosenbaum's edition.

Books entirely on *The Ambassadors*: A. Bellringer, *The Ambassadors* (London, 1984); A. Stone, ed., *Twentieth Century Interpretations of The Ambassadors* (Englewood Cliffs, N. J., 1969). Bellringer's book contains an excellent bibliography.

Books: C. Anderson, *Person, Place, and Thing* (Durham, N. C., 1977), 330–84; I. Bell, ed., *Henry James* (London, 1984), 98–113; N. Bradbury, *Henry James* (Oxford, 1979), 36–71; Chatman, *Later Style*; Fogel, *Henry James,* 14–48; Goode, ed., *Air of Reality,* 219–43; R. Hocks, *Henry James* (Chapel Hill), 152–83; C. Kaston, *Imagination and Desire* (New Brunswick, N. J., 1984), 82–108; J. Phelan, *World From Words* (Chicago, 1981), 43–66; Samuels, *Ambiguity,* 194–207; G. Sarotte, *Like a Brother, Like a Lover* (Garden City, N. Y., 1978), 197–211; F. Stanzel, *Narrative Situations in the Novel,* trans. J. Pusack, (Bloomington, 1971), 92–120; Wagenknecht, *Novels,* 182–

99; P. Weinstein, *Henry James* (Cambridge, Mass., 1971), 121–64; Yeazell, *Language and Knowledge,* 21–26, 28–31, 52–54, 60–62, 67–76.

Essays discussing revisions: Bellringer, *The Ambassadors,* 68-72; Rosenbaum, ed., *The Ambassadors,* 346–67.

General essays: L. Barnett, "Speech in *The Ambassadors:* Woollett and Paris as Linguistic Communities," *Novel* 16 (1983):215–29; E. T. Bender, "'The Question of His Own French': Dialect and Dialectic in *The Ambassadors,*" *Henry James Review* 5 (1984):128–134; L. Berkove, "Henry James and Sir Walter Scott: A 'Virtuous Attachment,'" *Studies in Scottish Literature* 15 (1980):43–52; D. Bock, "From Reflective Narrators to James: The Coloring Medium of the Mind," *Modern Philology* 76 (1979):259–72; E. Burde, "'*The Ambassadors* and the Double Vision of Henry James," *Essays in Literature* 4 (1977):59–77; J. Cherniak, "Henry James as Moralist," *Centennial Review* 16 (Winter, 1972):105–21; M. Cross, "'To Find the Names': *The Ambassadors,*" *Papers in Language and Literature* 19 (1983):402–18; S. Greenstein, "*The Ambassadors*: The Man of Imagination Encaged and Provided for," *Studies in the Novel* 9 (1977):137–53; Q. Grigg, "The Novel in *John Gabriel Borkman*: Henry James's *The Ambassadors,*" *Henry James Review* 1 (1980):211–18; J. Halverson, "Late Manner," *Sewanee Review* 79 (1971):214–31; C. Lohmann, "Jamesian Irony and the American Sense of Mission," *Texas Studies in Literature and Language* 16 (1974):329–47; R. Long, "*The Ambassadors* and the Genteel Tradition: James's Correction of Hawthorne and Howells," *New England Quarterly* 42 (1969):44–64; J. Miller, Jr., "Henry James on Reality," *Critical Inquiry* 2 (Spring 1976):585–604; E. Nettels, "*The Ambassadors* and the Sense of the Past," *Modern Language Quarterly* 31 (1970):220–35; D. Robinson, "James and Emerson: The Ethical Context of *The Ambassadors,*" *Studies in the Novel* 10 (1978):431–46; P. Rosenzweig, "James's 'Special-Green Vision': *The Ambassadors* as Pastoral," *Studies in the Novel* 13 (1981):367–87; S. Sacks, "Novelists as Storytellers," *Modern Philology* 73 (1976):597–609; W. Thomas, "The Author's Voice in *The Ambassadors,*" *Journal of Narrative Technique* 1 (1971):108–21; A. Tintner, "Balzac's 'Madame Firmiani' and James's *The Ambassadors,*" *Comparative Literature* 25 (1973):128–35; T. Tomlinson, "An American Strength: James's *The Ambassadors,*" *Critical Review* (Melbourne) 17 (1974):38–58; W. Veeder, "Strether and the Language of Transcendence," *Modern Philology* 68 (1971):116–32; J. Ward, "*The Ambassadors* as a Conversion Experience," *Southern Review* 5, n.s. (1969):350–74; J. Warner, " 'In View of Other Matters': The Religious Dimension of *The Ambassadors,*" *Essays in Literature* 4 (1977):78–94.

2. The many reviews of the novel were, in general, more positive than those provoked by *The Wings of the Dove.* Methuen published 3,500 copies of the one-volume novel in England and Harper issued 4,000 copies in the United States.

3. S. P. Rosenbaum's edition, which collates James's four versions of *The Ambassadors,* is the best edition of the novel.

4. *Notebooks,* 292.

5. The letter is quoted in H. Montgomery Hyde, *Henry James at Home* (New York, 1969), 99.

6. For Tintner, who focuses on the positive aspects of the Marie de Vionnet–Chad Newsome affair, *"The Ambassadors* is one of James's great tributes to Balzac, for the central situation, the classical civilizing liaison, is a distillation of what James learned from Balzac's variations on this subject—as exhibited in many of the volumes of *La Comèdie Humaine* as well as in "Madame Firmiani" ("Balzac's 'Madame Firmiani,'" 134). Most recently, Grigg, "The Novel in *John Gabriel Borkman,"* argues for the influence of Ibsen's play on several aspects of the novel, most significantly the implications of the younger man–older woman affair.

7. Long, *"The Ambassadors,"* argues that James's suggestions about the cultural causes of Strether's problems in responding fully to the environment of Paris—his New England sense of duty, his tendency toward abstraction and ambivalence about sexual energy—were influenced by his desire to improve upon Hawthorne's *Blithdale Romance* and Howells' *Indian Summer.* For Edel, "the novel spoke for the central myth of Henry James's life. James had long before made up his mind that his choice of Europe was wise, that . . . the U.S.A. could not offer him the sense of freedom he had won for himself abroad. Woollett was all constraint—it was rigid" *(The Master,* 78).

8. In an extremely influential comment in *The Great Tradition,* Leavis asserts, *"The Ambassadors* . . . produces an effect of disproportionate 'doing'— of a technique the subtleties and elaborations of which are not sufficiently controlled by a feeling for value and significance in living. What, we ask, is this, symbolized by Paris, that Strether feels himself to have missed in his own life? . . . Is it anything adequately realized?" (438).

9. F. W. Dupee, *Henry James,* 246. Hocks believes that Strether becomes an almost perfect pragmatist because of his "pragmatic cordiality to multiple meaning and awareness" and because of his willingness to continually "reconstruct" other characters. *(Henry James,* 171).

10. Sally Sears, *The Negative Imagination* (Ithaca, N. Y., 1968).

11. At least one critic (Sarotte, *Like a Brother*) believes that Strether's attraction to Chad is homosexual and that this feeling mirrors James's own sexual orientation.

12. Richards suggests that "We sometimes feel that the narrator is running a kind of three-legged race with the hero strapped onto his leg like a mute, but recording witness" (in *Art of Reality,* ed. Goode, 222).

13. Stanzel suggests that it will often depend upon the reader as to what will be considered authorial; perhaps a "biased epithet," for example, may be regarded by some readers as "authorial intrusion." If so, these readers will concretize in their imaginations an "authorial narrative situation" *(Narrative Situations,* 92).

14. In a recent, deconstructionist reading of *The Ambassadors,* Ellman

writes, "James's prose refuses to save meaning. . . . Rather than express the message, meanings twinkle, tremble, merge and deliquesce" (in *Henry James*, ed. Bell, 104). This is not quite true: James is not Roland Barthes. Although Lambert Strether, like his creator, has by the end of *The Ambassadors* become fascinated by Paris' "welter of signification," he also needs "single meaning" (ibid., 102). He therefore must go home.

Chapter Seven

   1.. The information derives primarily from S. Vincec's critical "'Poor Flopping Wings'": The Making of Henry James's *The Wings of the Dove*," *Harvard Library Bulletin* 24 (1976):60–93; and D. Crowley and R. Hocks, eds., *The Wings of the Dove* (New York, 1978), 408-11; hereafter this edition will be cited in the text.
   For secondary literature see the following.
   Books: Anderson, *Person, Place, and Thing*, 173–219; Bell, ed., *Henry James*, 82–97; Bradbury, *Henry James*, 72–122; P. Brooks, *The Melodramatic Imagination* (New Haven, 1976), 179–93; R. Caserio, *Plot, Story and the Novel* (Princeton, 1979), 211–25; S. Donadio, *Nietzsche, Henry James and the Artistic Will* (New York, 1978), 130–34; Fogel, *Henry James*, 49–84; V. Fowler, *Henry James's American Girl* (Madison, Wisc., 1984), 83–105, Goode, ed., *Air of Reality*, 244–300; Graham, *Henry James*, 160–232; Hocks, *Henry James*, 188–96; Maves, *Sensuous Pessimism*, 108–17; J. Meyers, *Painting and the Novel* (Manchester, 1975), 19–30; O'Neill, *Workable Design*, 105–31; J. Rowe, *Henry Adams and Henry James* (Ithaca, N. Y., 1976), 166–97; Samuels, *Ambiguity*, 61–72; Stowe, *Balzac*, 130–70; Wagenknecht, *Eve*, 153–69, 181–87; Wagenknecht, *Novels*, 208–17; Winner, *Henry James*, 66–67, 81–85; Yeazell, *Language and Knowledge*, 51–63, 76–84.
   Essays discussing revisions: Crowley and Hocks, *The Wings of the Dove*, 411–21; Vincec, "Poor Flopping Wings"; and Vincec, "A Significant Revision in *The Wings of the Dove*," *Review of English Studies* 23 (1972):58–61.
   General essays: M. Bell, "Jamesian Being," *Virginia Quarterly Review* 52 (1976):115–32; A. Bellringer, "*The Wings of the Dove*: The Main Image," *Modern Language Review* 74 (1979):12–25; Cherniak, "Henry James," 105–21; M. Hartsock, "Time for Comedy: The Late Novels of Henry James," *English Studies* 56 (1975):114–28; K. Komar, "Language and Character Delineation in *The Wings of the Dove*," *Twentieth Century Literature* 29 (1983):471–87; J. Korenman, "Henry James and the Murderous Mind," *Essays in Literature* 4 (1977):199–211; R. C. McLean, " 'Love by the Doctor's Direction': Disease and Death in *The Wings of the Dove*," *Papers on Language and Literature* 8, supp. (1972):128–48; G. Sebouhian, "The Transcendental Imagination of Merton Denscher," *Modern Language Studies* 5 (1975):35–45; W. Stein, "*The Wings of the Dove*: James's Eucharist of *Punch*," *Centennial Review* 21 (1977):236–60;

R. Thorberg, "*Germaine,* James's *Notebooks,* and *The Wings of the Dove,*" *Comparative Literature* 22 (1970):254–64; A. Tintner, "Henry James and the Symbolist Movement in Art," *Journal of Modern Literature* 7 (1979):397–415; J. Ward, "Henry James and Graham Greene," *Henry James Review* 1 (1979):10–23.

2. *The Wings of the Dove* was the first James work of international long fiction to appear in almost fifteen years (*The Reverberator* had begun serialization in February 1888). Perhaps surprisingly, few of the many reviews of the novel made reference to its international theme, so if James had hoped to capitalize on his early reputation (or notoriety) for handling this theme, he must have been disappointed. Although many of the reviewers did not like the novel, some were also willing (a bit grudgingly, in the United States) to acknowledge James's skill, even greatness. Moreover, several of the responses provoked by the novel were superbly and intelligently appreciative, and are still well worth reading (e.g., the article by Howells in the Norton critical edition, 483–87).

3. Many critics point to parallels between Milly's character and James's positive memories of his cousin. In a recent feminist reading, however, Fowler stresses James's supposed ambivalence (*Henry James*) (it was fortunate Milly died young because her passion for life would have found no outlet in America); Fowler then goes on to characterize her as a pathetic victim of her male-dominated American culture whose only real identity is achieved through illness.

4. Several critics have observed Shakespearean qualities (and particular parallels to *The Tempest, Macbeth* and *Othello*). Other possible sources suggested by critics are the non-Wagnerian Tristan and Isolde, "The Fall of the House of Usher" (because Milly haunts Denscher), *La Traviata,* Edward About's *Germaine,* Browning's "In a Balcony" and symbolic dramatists such as Maeterlinck and symbolic artists (Stein, observes in Milly a parody of pre-Raphaelite models akin to the parodies appearing in *Punch*).

5. Some critics have been bothered by the novel's supposed resemblance to allegory. Hocks's *Henry James* contains an unusually insightful discussion of the problems caused by the existence of *The Wings of the Dove* in a generic no-man's land between fairy tale, romance, and realistic novel.

6. The critical consensus about Denscher is that he is a basically nice, but weak and passive man who at the last is more or less redeemed by Milly's generosity.

7. For Rowe, *Henry Adams,* the Christian echoes "call into question all systems of metaphysical order as absolute sources for meaning" (176).

8. About the meaning of the Bronzino scene, Bradbury writes that what "might have been a definitive exercise, finding the perfect image for the heroine and thus framing her in the narrative, is turned instead into the active negation of such procedures, through the assertion of difference and the celebration of absence" (in *Henry James,* ed. Bell, 94).

Chapter Eight

1. There were several good reviews of *The Golden Bowl* in England (one reviewer even lamenting that it was not "double its length"! See Gard, ed., *Henry James*, 380). Moreover, it also sold relatively well: over some years there were two more impressions, making it the largest seller of any James English edition except for *Hawthorne*. In the United States, the novel quickly went through four editions, primarily, one suspects, because during James's trip he was the "literary lion of the hour," as the *New York Sun* reported. Although the novel was often mentioned and although many reviewers referred to James's fame, most were unenthusiastic.

For secondary literature see the following.

Books entirely devoted to *The Golden Bowl*: R. Normann, *The Insecure World of Henry James's Fiction* (London, 1982); R. Wilson, *Henry James's Ultimate Narrative* (St. Lucia, 1981). Wilson's study contains a thorough bibliography.

Books: Q. Anderson, *The Imperial Self* (New York, 1971), 166–200; P. Armstrong, *The Phenomenology of Henry James* (Chapel Hill, N. C., 1983), 136–86; Caserio, *Plot, Story and the Novel*, 211–25; Donadio, *Nietzsche*, 244–54; Fogel, *Henry James*, 85–137; Fowler, *Henry James's American Girl*, 108–40; Goode, ed., *Air of Reality*, 301–62; Kaston, *Imagination*, 121–79; Maves, *Sensuous Pessimism*, 125–49; D. Mull, *Henry James's "Sublime Economy"* (Middletown, Conn., 1973), 116–76; C. Porter, *Seeing and Being* (Middletown, Conn., 1981), 121–64; R. Posnock, *Henry James* (Athens, Ga., 1985), 153–87; Rowe, *Henry Adams*, 198–225; Samuels, *Ambiguity*, 210–26; Seltzer, *Henry James*, 59–95; Sicker, *Love*, 148–68; P. Stowell, *Literary Impressionism, James and Checkhov* (Athens, Ga., 1980), 221–39; Wagenknecht, *Eve*, 153–90; Wagenknecht, *Novels*, 218–37; Weinstein, *Henry James*, 164–94; Winner, *Henry James*, 153–69; Yeazell, *Language and Knowledge*, passim.

General essays: Cox; D. Craig, "The Indeterminacy of the End: Maggie Verver and the Limits of the Imagination," *Henry James Review* 3 (1982):133–44; S. Dougherty, "*The Golden Bowl*: Balzac, James, and the Rhetoric of Power," *Texas Studies in Literature and Language* 24 (1982):68–82; M. Hartsock, "Unintentional Fallacy: Critics and *The Golden Bowl*," *Modern Language Quarterly* 35 (1974):272–88; L. Levy, "*The Golden Bowl* and 'The Voice of Blood,'" *Henry James Review* 1 (1980):154–63; A. Ling, "The Pagoda Image in *The Golden Bowl*," *American Literature* 46 (1974):383–88; A. Mazzella, "'The Illumination that Was All for the Mind': The BBC Video Adaptation of *The Golden Bowl*," *Henry James Review* 2 (1981):213–27; D. Mogen, "Agonies of Innocence: The Governess and Maggie Verver," *American Literary Realism* 9 (1976):231–42; E. Nettels, "Henry James and the Idea of Race," *English Studies* 59 (1978):35–47; M. Nussbaum, "Flawed Crystals: James's *The Golden Bowl* and Literature as Moral Philosophy," *New Literary History* 15 (1983):25–47; M. Reynolds, "Counting the Costs: The Infirmity of Art and *The Golden*

Bowl," Henry James Review 6 (1984):15–26; B. Reddick, "The Control of Distance in *The Golden Bowl," Modern British Literature* 1 (1976):46–55; C. Sklenicka, "Henry James's Evasion of Ending in *The Golden Bowl," Henry James Review* 4 (1982):50–60; M. Torgovnick, "Gestural Pattern and Meaning in *The Golden Bowl," Twentieth Century Literature* 26 (1980):445–57; C. Torsney, "Prince Amerigo's Borgia Heritage," *Henry James Review* 2 (1981):126–31; R. Wallace, "Maggie Verver: Comic Heroine," *Genre* 6 (1973):404–15; C. Wessel, "Strategies for Survival in James's *The Golden Bowl," American Literature* 55 (1983):576–90.

2. *The Golden Bowl,* New York edition, vols. 23 and 24 (New York, 1909), 130–31, hereafter cited in the text.

3. *Notebooks,* 188.

4. Ibid., 233.

5. Edel refers to the "eroticism of the novelist's letters to his acolytes" (such as Persse and the young sculptor, Hendrik Andersen), and surmises that "James found in his relationship with Persse what he did not find with Andersen, the serenity that enabled him to make *The Golden Bowl* . . . a work unique among all his novels" (*The Master,* 191).

6. In a brilliant article, Cox ("Henry James") asserts that "What James accomplished in *The Golden Bowl* was simply everything": he made of the fairy tale a "novel of the richest consciousness"; he combined the incest theme (the heart of the romance) with adultery (the heart of the novel); he assimilated the "sentimental novel of seduction into the novel of manners."

7. King James Version, Ecclesiastes 12:6. C.f. the following lines from Blake's "Book of Thel": "Can wisdom be kept in a silver rod, / Or love in a golden bowl.'"

8. "The Story In It," in *The Complete Tales of Henry James,* vol. 9, ed. Leon Edel (London, 1964), 315.

9. The articles on Balzac, Flaubert, Zola, and D'Annunzio were collected in *Notes on Novelists* (London, 1914).

10. Dougherty ("*The Golden Bowl*") observes James's attempt to improve upon Balzac's *Cousine Bette* by creating a central character who combines "magnificent virtue and magnificent power." For Dougherty, however, "the rhetoric of love and the rhetoric of power are not fully compatible" (75), which helps explain the supposed problems in James's treatment of Maggie Verver.

11. Like each of the other three major characters, Charlotte has stimulated passionate, provocative, and multifarious critical responses. These range from the attitude of E. Owen, "'The Given Appearance' of Charlotte Verver," *Essays in Criticism* 13 (1963):364–74, who writes that "To the last Charlotte is clever, dangerous and brilliantly evil," to that of J. Kimball, "Henry James's Last Portrait of a Lady: Charlotte Stant in *The Golden Bowl," American Literature* 28 (1957):449–68, for whom Charlotte is the tragic heroine. Most would probably agree with Blackmur, who asserts in his 1952 introduction

to the Grove Press text that Charlotte "is no cheap predatory animal, though inhabited by one" (xiii).

12. In John Clair's ingenious but unconvincing reading of this relationship, Amerigo and Charlotte merely pretend to be lovers so as to provoke Maggie's jealousy and break up her unhealthy friendship with Adam. See *The Ironic Dimension of Henry James* (Pittsburgh, 1965), 79–102.

13. Yeazell (*Language and Knowledge*) suggests that Colonel Bob's gruff, skeptical responses to Fanny's interpretive flights are analogous to the comments made about James's fiction by his brother William.

14. Most critics observe in Maggie a flawed, but essentially good character (at the novel's beginning) who eventually becomes a kind of redemptive heroine; some readers attack her, however, and discern in her faults either unrecognized or not acknowledged by James.

15. Of the bowl, Peter Garrett writes, "Its significance may owe something to such extrinsic factors as allusions to the Bible or Blake, but it owes much more to the meanings it acquires at different moments for several of the characters" (*Scene and Symbol From George Eliot to James Joyce* [New Haven, 1969], 153).

16. There are almost as many good (and conflicting) interpretations of the enigmatic Adam Verver as there are of his daughter. Of those critics who observe primarily satire in Adam's supposedly naive dream for American City, Hartsock remarks, "I must remember that 'unreality' the next time I visit the National Gallery, the Chicago Arts Institute, the Folger Library, or other repositories of great art available to people too poor to afford even the special M.L.A. airfare to Europe!" ("Unintentional Fallacy," 275).

17. The syntax does not make clear whether Maggie imagines Charlotte to be Ariadne, or herself. Rowe, assuming the latter, argues that, ironically, "Her art transforms her into the minotaur -- the destructive element itself" (*Henry Adams*, 219).

18. To Mull, "those muted, elliptical conversations between Adam and Maggie . . . point toward a recognition of guilt, coexisting with an attempt by each to conceal from the other the wounding fact of knowledge" (*Henry James's "Sublime Economy,"* 153).

19. To most critics, the Prince's seemingly dismissive reference to Charlotte as "stupid" signals a definite callousness. Perhaps, however, as he muses about Charlotte and laments her inability to "know" Maggie, the Prince suddenly remembers a prediction made by Charlotte at Matcham, just as they prepare to leave for Gloucester: "Ah for things I mayn't want to know I promise you shall find me stupid" (1:363). Perhaps, therefore, rather than insulting her by calling her "stupid," Amerigo is paying tacit and ironic tribute to Charlotte's strategy for survival. As he says to Maggie, "what I mean is that she's not, as you perceive her, unhappy" (2:348).

20. Responses to the enigmatic ending have been as diverse as to the rest of the novel. From Porter's Marxian point of view, for example, "The

Prince's personal, single self is nowhere in evidence in the novel's closing scene" because he is now "engulfed by that market place, whose high priestess he now worships" (*Seeing and Being*, 147). Sicker writes, "*The Golden Bowl* concludes in an atmosphere of emotional claustrophobia and despair; the lovers draw closer together until their embrace ends in a kind of blackout" (*Lover*, 167). For Donadio, however, the ending "embraces two antithetical and ostensibly irreconcilable possibilities, for it represents a triumph in the actual world as well as a triumph of the spirit" (*Nietzsche* 252). Ward suggests that the "art" of Maggie Verver "is process and act, not achieved finality. The salvation of her marriage is the struggle to preserve it" (*The Search for Form*, 216).

Chapter Nine

1. See R. Hewitt, "Henry James's *The American Scene*: Its Genesis and Its Reception," *Henry James Review* 1 (1980):179–96.

2. Quoted by Edel in *Henry James*, 617. James first delivered the lecture as the commencement address at Bryn Mawr in the spring of 1905. It was later published as part of a series of articles on American speech and manners in *Harper's Bazaar*. Most of the articles were written after he had completed *The American Scene*.

3. For a discussion of how finances influenced the structure of the New York Edition, see M. Anesko, "Friction with the Market: The Publication of Henry James's New York Edition," *New England Quarterly* 56 (1983):354–81.

4. Both *The High Bid* and *The Outcry* were given London revivals in the late 1960s.

5. For a discussion of *The Finer Grain* as a short story cycle, see the preface to the reprint edited by W. Martin and W. Ober and published by Scholars Reprints & Facsimiles. Their preface also compares *The Finer Grain* to earlier collections with a loose thematic organization such as *A Passionate Pilgrim, and Other Tales* (1875) and the short-story volumes of the New York Edition. James's other published short stories were "The Jolly Corner" and "Julia Bride." He also contributed a chapter entitled "The Married Son" to the collaborative twelve-chapter novel, *The Whole Family*, which was serialized in 1906–7 and published in 1908.

6. Edel, *Henry James*, 689.

7. John Kimmey, "The 'London' Book," *Henry James Review* 1 (1979):67.

8. Percy Lubbock published material relating to *The Ivory Tower* as volume 25 of the New York Edition in 1917.

9. Percy Lubbock published the almost four "books" and extensive notes relating to *The Sense of the Past* as volume 26 of the New York Edition in 1917.

Selected Bibliography

PRIMARY SOURCES

This bibliography is selective, citing only the long, finished novels published after *The Bostonians*. Complete information relating to James's mammoth, heterogeneous publication may be found in *A Bibliography of Henry James,* 3rd ed., ed. Leon Edel, Dan Laurence, and James Rambeau (Oxford: Clarendon Press, 1982).

The Princess Casamassima. Atlantic Monthly, September 1885–October 1886. First book edition: London: Macmillan, 1886. Rev. ed. New York Edition, vols. 5–6. New York: Scribner's, 1907–9.

The Tragic Muse. Atlantic Monthly, January 1889–May 1890. First book edition: Boston: Houghton, Mifflin; London: Macmillan, 1890. Rev. ed. New York Edition, vols. 7–8. New York: Scribner's 1907–9.

The Awkward Age. Harper's Weekly, 1 October 1898–7 January 1899. First book edition: London: William Heinemann; New York: Harper, 1899. Rev. ed. New York Edition, vol. 9. New York: Scribner's 1907–9.

The Wings of the Dove. New York: Charles Scribner's Sons; Westminster: Archibald Constable, 1902. Rev. ed. New York Edition, vols. 19–20. New York: Scribner's, 1907–9.

The Ambassadors. North American Review, January–December 1903. London: Methuen; New York: Harper, 1903. Rev. ed. New York Edition, vols. 21–22. New York: Scribner's 1907–9.

The Golden Bowl. New York: Charles Scribner's Sons, 1904; London: Methuen, 1905. Rev. ed. New York Edition, vols. 23–24. New York: Scribner's, 1907–9.

SECONDARY SOURCES

This section annotates only selected post-1970 books and articles closely related to the later novels. Of the many pre-1970 works annotated by Robert L. Gale ("Henry James," in *Eight American Authors,* ed. James Woodress [New York, 1971], 321–75), particularly important are Edel's biography, Warren's general article, and books by Cargill, Dupee, Holland, Matthiessen, and Putt.

Anderson, Charles. *Person, Place, and Thing in the Novels of Henry James.* Durham, N.C.: Duke University Press, 1977. Long, sometimes plodding, often useful chapters about how "things"—houses, for example—function.

Bradbury, Nicola. *Henry James: The Later Novels.* Oxford: Clarendon Press, 1979. Stylistically dense, sensitive analyses of fiction's unsettling relationship with reader.

Brooks, Peter. *The Melodramatic Imagination: Balzac, Henry James, Melodrama, and the Mode of Excess.* New Haven: Yale University Press, 1976. Convincing study of how James's "melodramas of manners" suggest ultimate values while avoiding allegory.

Caserio, Robert. *Plot, Story and the Novel.* Princeton: Princeton University Press, 1979. Excellent iconoclastic chapter stressing the value of action (not passivity) for James's late characters.

Chatman, Seymour. *The Later Style of Henry James.* New York: Barnes & Noble, 1972. Excellent short study of James's style and its implications.

Cherniak, Judith. "Henry James as Moralist: The Case of the Late Novels." *Centennial Review* 16 (Winter 1972):105–21. Stimulating essay attributing ambiguity to James's ironic treatment of inevitable conflict between the romantic and the real.

Cox, James. "Henry James: The Politics of Internationalism." *Southern Review* 8, n.s. (1972):493–506. Superb article focusing on *Princess* but considering also political implications of James's life and international fiction.

Donadio, Stephen. *Nietzsche, Henry James and the Artistic Will.* New York: Oxford University Press, 1978. Exciting reading paralleling James's and Nietzsche's interest in the "tangled, shifting relationship of selfhood, selfishness, and selflessness."

Fogel, Daniel Mark. *Henry James and the Structure of the Romantic Imagination.* Baton Rouge: Louisiana State University Press, 1981. Persuasive discussions tracing working-out of "spiral dialectic" concept in characters' quests for experience.

Fowler, Virginia. *Henry James's American Girl: The Embroidery on the Canvas.* Madison: University of Wisconsin Press, 1984. Good feminist study of fictional use and cultural implications of James's "American Girl."

Gill, Richard. *Happy Rural Seat: The English Country House and the Literary Imagination.* New Haven: Yale University Press, 1972. Perceptive long chapter on sources and functions of James's country houses.

Goode, John, ed. *The Air of Reality: New Essays on Henry James.* London: Methuen, 1972. Long, generally excellent essays on most James novels.

Graham, Kenneth. *Henry James: The Drama of Fulfillment.* London: Oxford

University Press, 1975. Marvellously appreciative discussions of search by James characters for fulfilling vocations.

Halverson, John. "Late Manner, Major Phase." *Sewanee Review* 79 (April–June 1971): 214–31. Discussion attacking "excessive suggestiveness" and subtlety of late style, but recognizing gain in moral depth.

Hocks, Richard H. *Henry James and Pragmatistic Thought: A Study of the Relationship between the Philosophy of William James and the Literary Art of Henry James.* Chapel Hill: University of North Carolina Press, 1974. Superb study of how Henry "unconsciously pragmatized."

Jacobson, Marcia. *Henry James and the Mass Market.* University: University of Alabama Press, 1983. Study outlining James's continual attempts to achieve popularity.

Kaston, Carren. *Imagination and Desire in the Novels of Henry James.* New Brunswick, N. J.: Rutgers University Press, 1984. Study of James's ambivalent treatment of quasi-artists who try to dominate world through imagination.

Margolis, Anne T. *Henry James and the Problem of Audience.* Ann Arbor: University of Michigan Press, 1985. Informative, sometimes reductive study of James's attempts to win both avant-garde and conventional audiences.

Maves, Carl. *Sensuous Pessimism: Italy in the Work of Henry James.* Bloomington: Indiana University Press, 1973. Excellent study of Italy's influence on and use in James's work.

Miller, James, Jr. "Henry James on Reality." *Critical Inquiry* 2 (Spring 1976):585–604. Incisive article emphasizing dangers of trying to pigeonhole James, given concern for freedom and individual consciousness.

O'Neill, John. *Workable Design: Action and Situation in the Fiction of Henry James.* Port Washington, N. Y.: Kennikat Press, 1973. Occasionally persuasive explanations of how James's interest in pattern and rhetorical effect influence his fiction.

Perosa, Sergio. *Henry James and the Experimental Novel.* Charlottesville: University of Virginia Press, 1978. Thoughtful discussions of mid-career and final Jamesian fictional experiments.

Posnock, Ross. *Henry James and the Problem of Robert Browning.* Athens: University of Georgia Press, 1985. Deconstructive account of James's early anxiety about and later conscious use of Browning.

Powers, Lyall. *Henry James and the Naturalist Movement.* Lansing: Michigan State University Press, 1971. Thorough examination of influence of French naturalistic fiction.

Rowe, John Carlos. *Henry Adams and Henry James: The Emergence of a Modern Consciousness.* Ithaca, N. Y.: Cornell University Press, 1976. Challenging interpretation stressing James's late distrust of fixed meaning (and characters and readers who demand it).

Samuels, Charles T. *The Ambiguity of Henry James.* Urbana: University of

Illinois Press, 1971. Stimulating, controversial judgments about effects on fiction of predeliction for innocent characters and renunciatory actions.

Schneider, Daniel. *The Crystal Cage: Adventures of the Imagination in the Fiction of Henry James.* Lawrence: Regents Press of Kansas, 1978. Provocative image study, focusing on tension between images of freedom and entrapment.

Seltzer, Mark. *Henry James and the Art of Power.* Ithaca, N. Y.: London: Cornell University Press, 1984. Study of how James's fiction "represses and acknowledges a discreet continuity between literary and political practices."

Sicker, Philip. *Love and the Quest for Identity in the Fiction of Henry James.* Princeton: Princeton University Press, 1980. Interpretation making James a pre-Lawrentian explorer of links between love and self-definition.

Stone, Donald D. *Novelists in a Changing World: Meredith, James, and the Transformation of English Fiction in the 1880's.* Cambridge, Mass.: Harvard University Press, 1972. Thoughtful, well-informed discussion of James's stretching of Victorian fictional conventions.

Stowe, William W. *Balzac, James, and the Realistic Novel.* Princeton: Princeton University Press, 1983. Stimulating discussion of how James's fiction challenges readers to continually create and constantly modify meaning.

Wagenknecht, Edward. *Eve and Henry James: Portraits of Women and Girls in His Fiction.* Norman: University of Oklahoma Press, 1978. Lively, well-informed discussion of critic's favorite Jamesian female characters.

———. *The Novels of Henry James.* New York: Frederick Ungar, 1983. Cantankerous, often simplistic, sometimes shrewd and useful survey.

Weinstein, Philip M. *Henry James and the Requirements of the Imagination.* Cambridge, Mass.: Harvard University Press, 1971. Often critical examination of way James treats conflict between character's desire to live in world and imagination.

Winner, Viola Hopkins. *Henry James and the Visual Arts.* Charlottesville: University Press of Virginia, 1970. Excellent historical and critical study of James's knowledge and use of visual arts.

Yeazell, Ruth Bernard. *Language and Knowledge in the Late Novels of Henry James.* Chicago: University of Chicago Press, 1976. Best recent study of late James, focusing lucidly on the implications of style.

Index